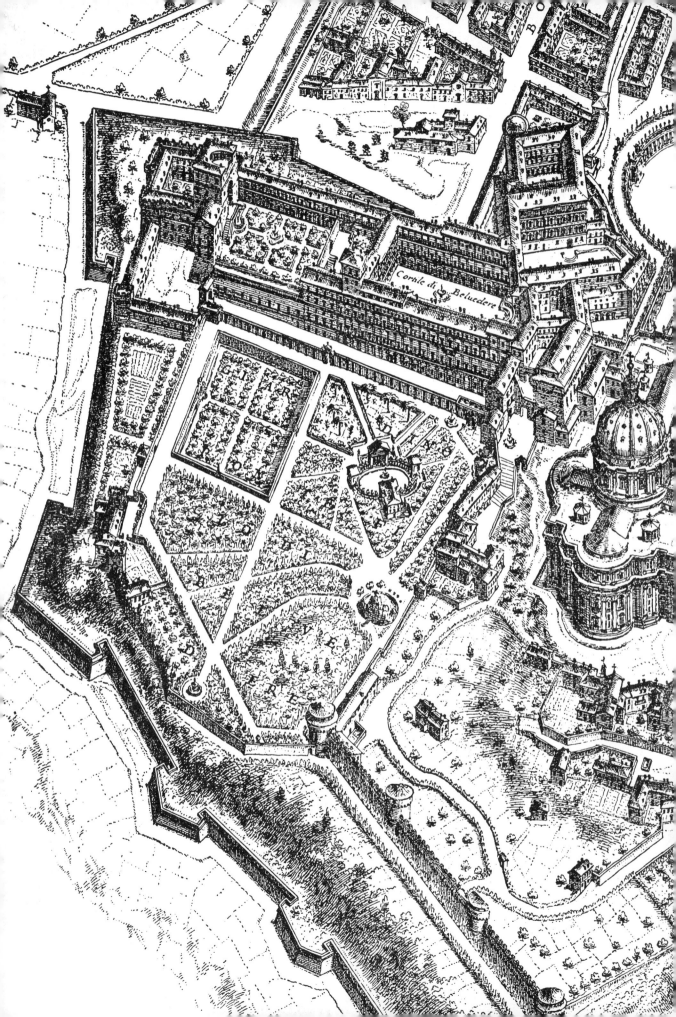

Cortile di Beluedere

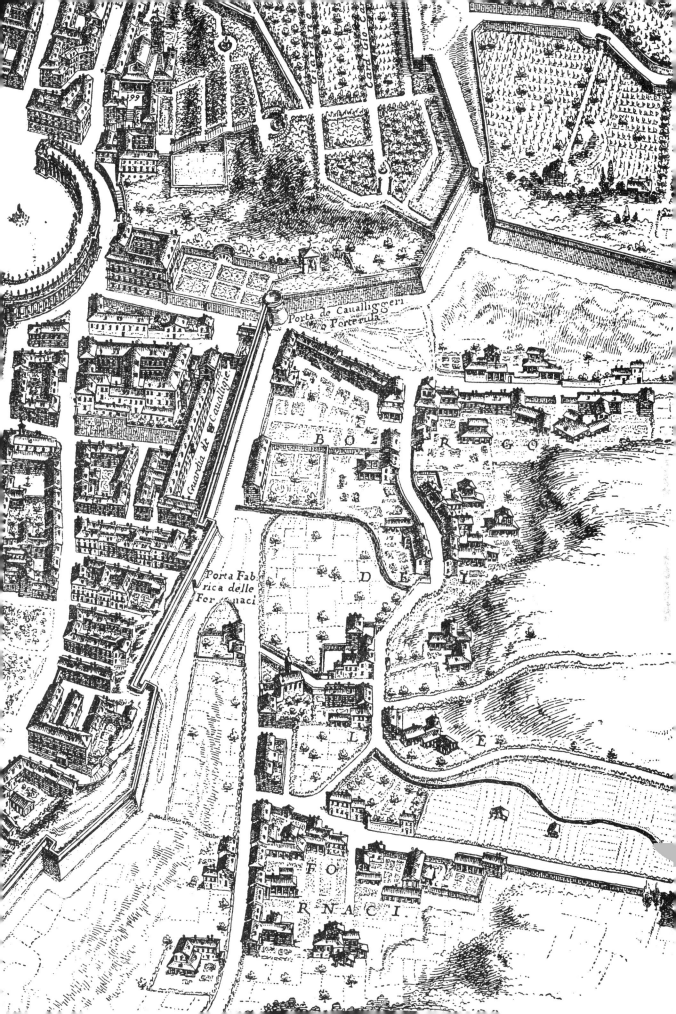

Porta de Caualliggeri
o Portezula

Guardia di SS.Caualligre

BORGO

Porta Fab
rica delle
For naci

DEL

L

E

FO

RNACI.

The Story of St. Peter's

Illustrated with photographs, prints, and with drawings by Richard Bergere

Dodd, Mead & Company
New York

The Story of St. Peter's

THEA AND RICHARD BERGERE

For Thea and Guy

Author's Note

On the following pages is an account of the origin and reconstruction of the Basilica of St. Peter in the Vatican which covers a period of thirteen and a half centuries, from the consecration of the first basilica, up to the time of the erection of the colonnades on the Piazza di San Pietro, which completed the edifice as it is seen today. Considerable research went into the text, for it is a work compiled from numerous facts — isolated and scattered through histories of Rome, art and architecture, and technical essays — arranged into a chronological, informative story of the building of St. Peter's. It includes few mentions of other parts of the Vatican, for we were solely concerned with presenting an understandable, concise record of the construction of St. Peter's; and by that same token, though it does contain a limited amount of historical background, it is not a history of Rome or the Papacy.

We wish to express our gratitude to C. J. McNaspy, S. J., for his advice in matters of accuracy. We would also like to thank Mr. Adolph K. Platzek of the Avery Architectural Library at Columbia University, Mr. Donald R. Allen of the Art Reference Bureau, Inc., Ancram, New York, and the Italian State Tourist Office, for having cooperated in supplying pictorial material for the preparation of this book. We appreciate, too, the courtesy extended to us by the staffs of the Queens Borough and New York Public Library systems.

Contents

Introduction

The mighty, majestic Basilica of St. Peter in the Vatican, famed as the climax building of the Renaissance, is the largest church in the world and undoubtedly the most magnificent in all Europe. Between 1506, when the cornerstone was laid, and 1626, when the present St. Peter's was consecrated, lies the impressive span of 120 years. During that long drawn out building period, and for generations afterwards as the interior was being completed, a number of illustrious architects and artists were associated with its design, construction, and adornment.

The first plans for the rebuilding of St. Peter's were drawn in 1454 by Alberti and Rossellino, who proposed a huge Latin-cross basilica. Fifty-two years later, Donato Bramante envisioned the church as a Greek cross with a great central dome, but his successors, Raphael, Peruzzi, and Antonio da Sangallo the Younger, made several alterations in the plan. Michelangelo returned to Bramante's Greek-cross form which he considered to be "clear, comprehensive, and luminous," although he simplified the scheme and redesigned the dome. Giacomo della Porta and Domenico Fontana constructed the dome twenty-six years after the death of Michelangelo, then Carlo Maderna extended the nave, which changed St. Peter's to a Latin cross, and added the façade. Finally, Giovanni Lorenzo Bernini, who contributed more toward the lavish decorations than any other individual, designed and erected the noble colonnades of the Piazza di San Pietro, the entrance court of the basilica.

St. Peter's, entirely hand-built, covers a total area of 227,070 square feet, well over five acres. Its internal length—almost an eighth of a mile—extends a distance of 613 feet from the bronze door at the main entrance to the western apse wall, and all of this enormous interior is richly finished in a profusion of fine colored marble, beautiful stucco work, and glorious mosaics.

9

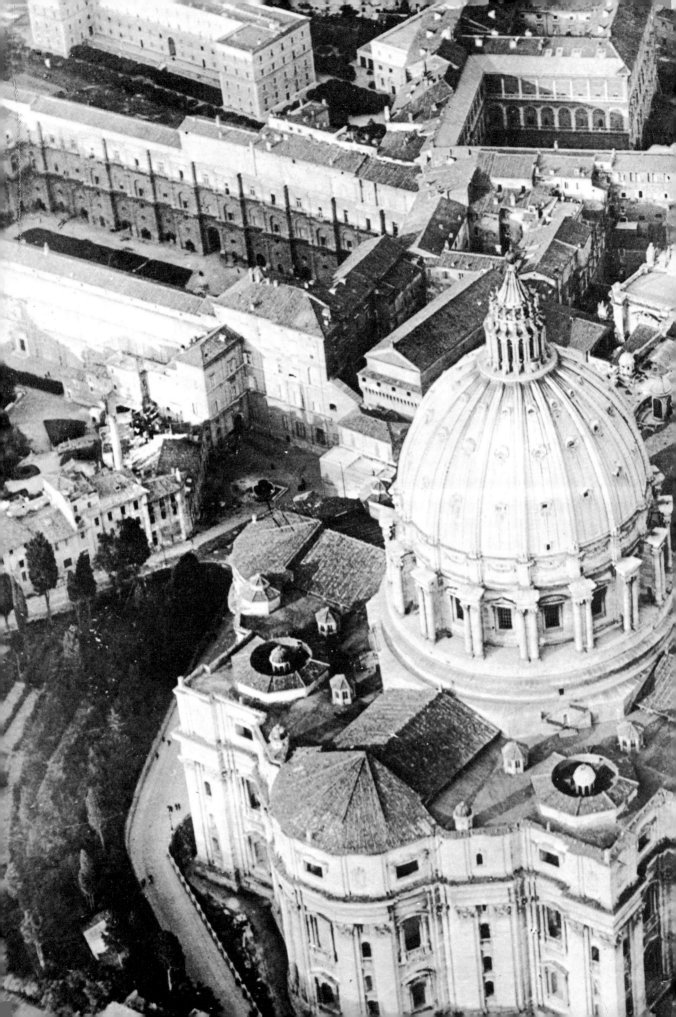

The massive exterior is of travertine with a giant order of Corinthian columns and pilasters over 90 feet tall, which support an entablature and an attic story, together almost 60 feet high. The colossal façade, 375 feet wide, rises to 167 feet. Monumental statues of the Saviour and the Apostles are surmounted on its balustrade, and an inscription, carved in bold Roman letters across the frieze, honors Pope Paul V who saw the front completed in 1612.

The crowning glory of St. Peter's is, of course, the splendid dome which soars over the crossing of the church, directly over the first Apostle's tomb. With its graceful lantern and 16-foot bronze cross, the dome attains an over-all height of 452 feet. It is Rome's most prominent landmark, the world-famous symbol of the Vatican City.

Detail from the bronze doors by Filarete (center portal of St. Peter's)

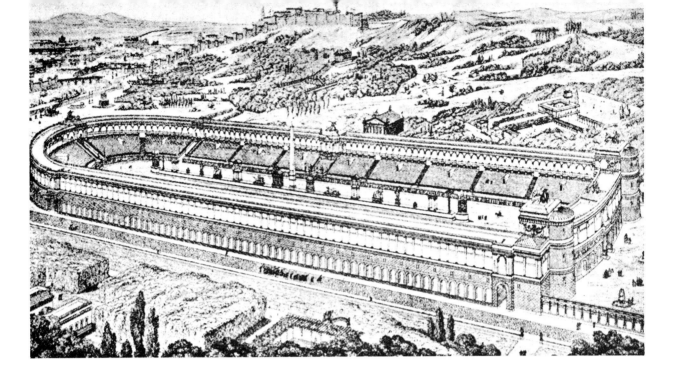

The Tomb of St. Peter

We know, from the history of the Church, that St. Peter, Prince of the Apostles and the first Pope, was martyred, probably A.D. 67. He suffered death by crucifixion—nailed to a cross, head downward—in the arena of the Circus of Nero.

Soon after the Apostle died, his body was claimed by fellow Christians and borne to a pagan cemetery, just a short distance north from the scene of his execution. There, on the steep slope of Vatican Hill, St. Peter was given a simple burial in a grave which, Vatican archaeologists concluded, must have been merely a trench, dug into the hillside and covered over with tiles. Though possibly unmarked by a tombstone or monument of any kind, the revered, simple gravesite was well known to early Christians who came to it almost continuously to pray.

About the middle of the second century, the number of pagan mausoleums in the Vatican cemetery had increased to such an extent that the Christians in Rome were concerned with the probability that, in time, additional tombs would encroach upon the burial site of St. Peter. Shortly thereafter (the date has been determined as between A.D. 160 and 170) they constructed a barrier—a reddish wall—to protect the sacred place, and with it they built an *Aedicula,* a shrine, above the grave.

13

Street of pagan tombs beneath St. Peter's

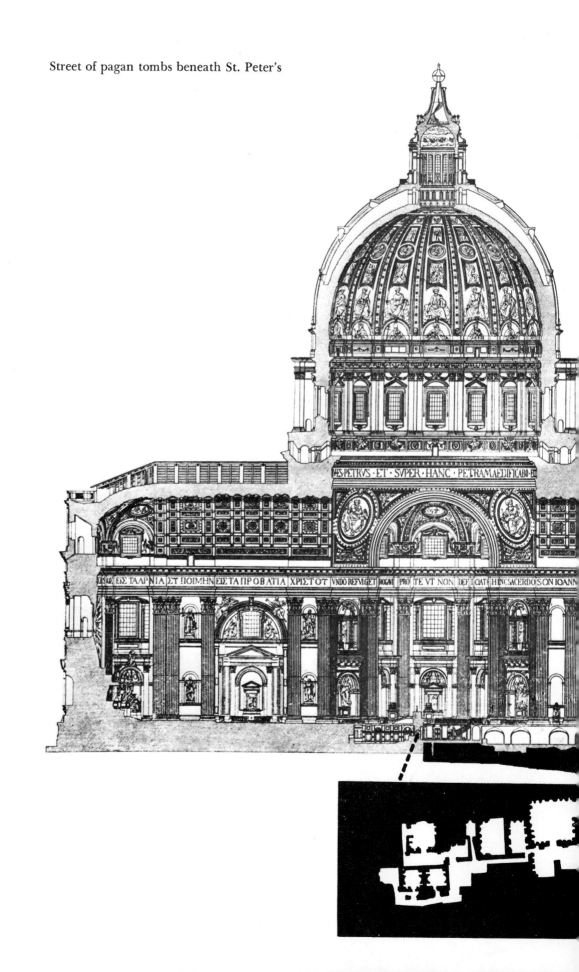

Until the reign of Pope Pius XII (1939-1958), all that was known about the Tomb of St. Peter was based on traditions handed down by the Church through the centuries. Emperor Constantine the Great, who granted Christians the freedom to worship in 313 and founded the first church of St. Peter in 324, had encased the Aedicula in masonry and sheathed it in marble and porphyry, a purple, sometimes red, rock formation embedded with crystalline masses. There were only fragmentary records of the shrine's original appearance, and there was no certainty that it still existed. However, in 1940, Pius XII permitted a team of archaeologists and engineers to excavate and explore the area beneath the Confessio and High Altar of the Basilica of St. Peter and the ancient monument was rediscovered. Through scientific examinations it was verified to be the actual Tomb of St. Peter —the "trophy" of the Apostle mentioned by Gaius, a Roman priest, who saw it on Vatican Hill about A.D. 200. The archaeological probing, which was conducted in secrecy for ten years, also revealed a street of pagan tombs beneath the ground level of the basilica that have since been made accessible to a limited number of privileged visitors and scholars.

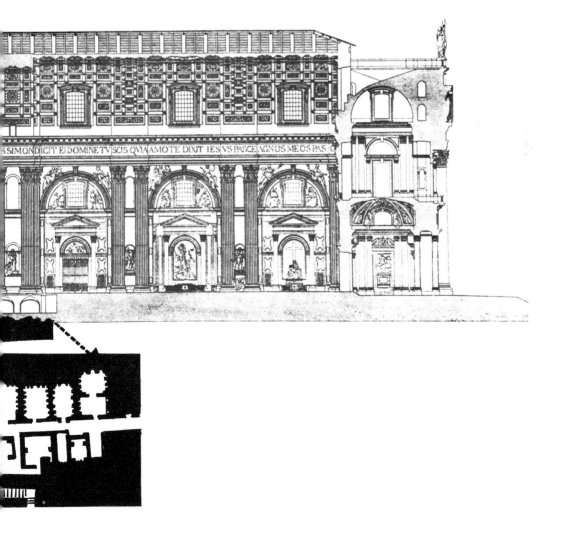

Above: Tomb beneath St. Peter's

Right: Aedicula of St. Peter's reconstructed by Vatican archaeologists

What remained of the Aedicula and the section of the red wall into which it had been embedded, enabled the Vatican researchers to build a full-scale representation of the monument as it must have looked shortly after its completion. The replica shows that the Aedicula had two niches above the ground (there was a third below) recessed into the wall and separated from each other by a horizontal slab of travertine. The heavy slab projected from the wall and was supported at its two outer corners by a pair of small marble columns that stood upon a travertine foundation slab. The upper niche was framed by two plain pilaster strips which carried a marble pediment. After its construction, the shrine was carefully tended. Eventually the ground-level niche and the walls adjoining it on either side were faced with marble, a block of marble covered the original foundation slab, and the shrine's small courtyard was paved with marble cubes.

16

Constantine's Basilica

The first St. Peter's, which existed for more than twelve centuries on the site now occupied by the present basilica, was only partly built when Pope Sylvester I (314-335) consecrated it in 326. Although its construction was well advanced before the death of Constantine the Great in 337, so much remained unfinished that the Emperor's son, Constans, was occupied with the direction of the work for twelve more years.

When Constantine, prompted by Pope Sylvester, made his decision to build a church to enshrine the Tomb of St. Peter, he planned a big basilica, 400 feet long, 230 feet wide, with a single apse at its western end to be erected over the Aedicula. It was a very challenging enterprise for his engineers because the venerated grave was situated in a section of the Vatican cemetery where the land sloped steeply on two sides—down to the east and south—curving towards the valley. To prepare the site, Constantine's workmen had to cut away part of the hillside north and west of the shrine, and at the same time, build up a massive terrace on the lower slopes. It is said that the Emperor himself carried away the first twelve baskets of earth from the western excavations in honor of the twelve Apostles.

Huge foundation walls of concrete, faced with alternating courses of brick, and brick with stone, were constructed along the main lines of the church. Then the area within those great boundaries, which encompassed numerous pagan tombs, was solidly packed (*congestio terrarum*) with clay and earth. Gradually the walls were built higher and higher until the entire structure, filled with over a million cubic feet of earth, was even with the ground level of St. Peter's tomb. When the enormous platform was completed, its southeast corner, based on the lowest point of the site, rose up to a height of 35 feet.

The plan illustrated on the following page, from Letarouilly & Simil, first printed in Paris in 1882, shows the present basilica in its relationship to Constantine's church, which in turn is partly superimposed over a diagram of the Circus of Nero. Drawings that are almost identical to this one appear in many old architectural publications, for, from the beginning of St. Peter's rebuilding and onward, it was a generally accepted belief that the church's south foundations had been set on the north wall of the abandoned stadium. During the excavations of 1940-1950, however, this long held theory was apparently disproved, for the archaeologists, searching for remains of Nero's wall, exposed part of the southwest foundation of the ancient church down to the soil on which it stood, and discovered that it was entirely of fourth century construction, not first century.

17

Plan of Constantine's basilica and the
present St. Peter's superimposed over
drawing of Nero's Circus

Constantine's basilica

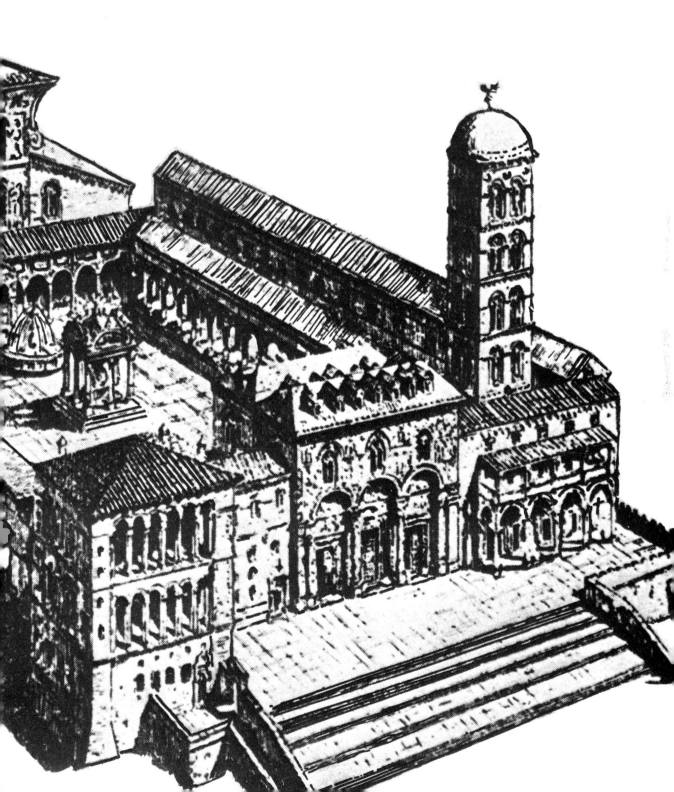

Constantine's church was built of brick and had a timber roof that was covered with tiles of brick, bronze, and lead. It was a spacious, five-aisled basilica, divided lengthwise by four long colonnades, each consisting of twenty-two marble columns of various designs. The two rows of columns that defined the wide middle aisle, or *nave*, supported lofty walls that rose higher than the low-pitched roofs over the side aisles. These walls, pierced midway to the top with many round-headed windows, formed the *clerestory* which illuminated the central area of the basilica. They were decorated with frescoes depicting scenes from the Gospels, and the panels between the windows were painted with elongated figures representing the twelve Apostles and several saints and martyrs.

A narrow transverse passage, called a *transept,* separated the side aisles and nave from the semi-circular apse at the west end. Originally this corridor was only as long as the width of the main body of the church, but at some later date it was extended by two terminal chapels which projected to the north and south, so that the building became T-shaped in plan.

Between the nave and transept, there was a great triumphal arch. It was adorned with a mosaic which portrayed Emperor Constantine offering a model of the basilica to Christ and St. Peter. The mosaic's inscription read: "Because under Thy leadership the world rose up triumphant to the skies, Constantine himself victorious, has founded this hall in Thy honor."

The Tomb of St. Peter stood on the chord of the apse, above the pavement of the basilica, its site dramatized by a large *baldacchino* or canopy, from which hung a golden crown-shaped lamp embellished with fifty dolphins. The lamp, no longer in existence, was said to have weighed 35 pounds and was listed in the *Book of Popes (Liber Pontificalis)* as one of the many splendid gifts of Constantine.

Four ornately carved spiral columns, set upon a low marble platform and fenced together by a balustrade, upheld an entablature and the plain arched ribs which formed the canopy above the shrine. These pure white marble columns, part of a group of six which the Emperor had brought from Greece, were about 15 feet tall and decorated with alternating bands of fluting and vine scroll. Their

Old St. Peter's, restored elevation

Artist's conception of baldacchino erected by Emperor Constantine

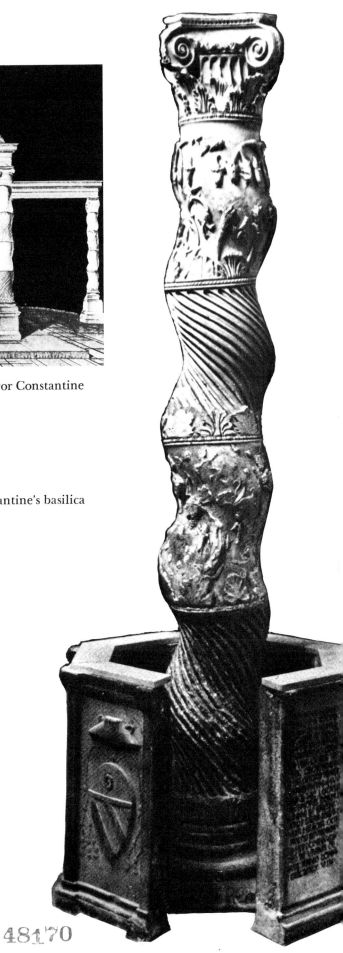

Spiral column from Constantine's basilica

curving shape was unusual for that period, and they may have been the first of their kind so designed. Toward the end of the Middle Ages, it was popularly believed that they had been taken from Solomon's Temple at Jerusalem.

The shrine itself, boxed within a protective casing of masonry, was covered in marble and trimmed at the corners with column-like strips of porphyry which carried a carved entablature. There was a niche recessed into its east front, divided by a horizontal ledge, with a cross in the upper half and a double gate below.

The oldest surviving pictorial representation of the shrine, as it appeared in Constantine's setting, was carved on the side of an ivory chest dating from the fifth century. It was found on Italy's Istrian peninsula near the province of Pola in 1906, and is now in the museum there. Despite its distorted perspective, the carving shows the shrine, the spiral columns, and the canopy with the hanging lamp in clear detail.

Pola Casket

Apse mosaic

This same ancient chest has, on its opposite, outer side, scenes from the mosaic which decorated the semi-dome of the apse behind the shrine. That colorful work depicted Christ in Majesty, seated between Sts. Peter and Paul, and flanked by two palm trees. Centered below was the Agnus Dei or Lamb of God, the emblem of Christ, with six sheep on either side which symbolized the twelve Apostles, and the cities of Bethlehem and Jerusalem. Beneath the pictorials, on a broad band of mosaic, was the inscription: "The seat of justice, the house of faith, the hall of modesty, such is that you see, the abode of all piety. It proclaims its joy and pride in the merits both of father and son, for both alike it honors as its founders."

There is no certainty as to where the main altar stood in the basilica during the fourth and fifth centuries. It is believed to have been a portable one that was probably placed beneath the canopy in front of the shrine when the Mass was to be celebrated on special church anniversaries and holy days. At other times the ceremonies were more likely to have been conducted in the nave, with the altar positioned near the great triumphal arch.

Worshipers attending services were restricted to the side aisles where they had to stand or kneel on the church's bare pavement. This custom remained through the centuries and is the reason why fixed benches or seats were never installed in any of the great churches of Rome. When Mass was not being said, visiting pilgrims were allowed to enter the precinct of the transept and permitted to pray at the balustrade of the baldacchino, in closer proximity to the venerated shrine.

23

At the east end of the nave and side aisles, the front of the church, there were five doorways which opened onto a wide columned entrance porch called the *narthex*. In it was a large marble statue of St. Peter which still exists, preserved in the grotto of the present basilica.

Adjoining the narthex was an open, rectangular colonnaded court, the *atrium*, in which there was a mosaic representing the Apostles in a boat and St. Peter walking on the waves to meet the Saviour. This monumental work, attributed to Giotto, is the restored *Navicella* that is now located over the entrance inside the portico of St. Peter's. A large fountain where the faithful cleansed themselves before going into church, stood in the center of the atrium sheltered by a dome. Its huge *pigna*, or pine cone, of bronze was later transferred by Pope Paul V (1605-1621) to a niche in the Belvedere courtyard of the Vatican Palace. The entrance to the atrium was a portico made up of units which were two and three stories high, with three central gates and a campanile on the north side. It was fronted by a broad flight of steps which led down to a vast piazza.

Two circular Roman mausoleums, with domed roofs of concrete, stood to the south of the basilica. They were connected together by a covered corridor, and the western one was joined directly to the left transept of the church. This mausoleum held the fifth-century tombs of Emperor Honorius and his wife, Maria, and possibly that of Theodosius II. It was converted into a chapel dedicated to St. Petronilla—St. Peter's "spiritual daughter"—who died in the first century. Her sarcophagus, a stone coffin, was placed there in 757. The second mausoleum, which had foundations dating from the second century, was made the Chapel of St. Andrew in honor of the brother of St. Peter. It later became the Chapel of Santa Maria della Febbre.

Although outwardly the brick and timber basilica remained unchanged through the centuries, it became increasingly grander within. Each year thousands of pilgrims brought offerings and royal benefactors enriched it with munificent gifts, so that in time it housed a wealth of precious metalwork, jewels and enamels, sculptured marble, stained glass, and frescoes.

But in the course of history barbarian raiders invaded Rome many times, and on these disastrous occasions, the marauders plundered the church and carried away most of its treasures. Alaric the Goth descended on Rome in the year 408, and a second foray was made in 410; Attila, King of the Huns, attacked in 452, but was successfully repulsed; then Genseric the Vandal leveled the city in 455; Totila the Goth ruined it in 546; and it was sacked by the Saracens in 846. Nevertheless, after each incursion, the devout salvaged and repaired what had been left in the church, and did what they could to restore its beauty with new paintings, mosaics, statuary, and other costly decorations.

24

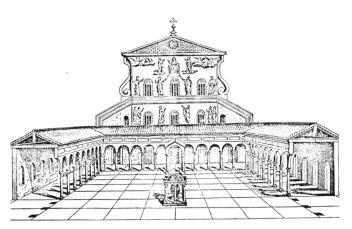

Left: Atrium of Constantine's basilica. Center right: Restored *Navicella*, attributed to Giotto. Center left: Bronze *pigna*.

Left: Façade of atrium

26

St. Peter's shrine grew more beautiful as successive popes added embellishments of gold and silver. Yet, though lavishly adorned, the marble monument was kept essentially the same as Constantine had designed it, and remained standing above the pavement of the church for all to see to the end of the sixth century.

Pope Gregory the Great (590-604) "made it possible to celebrate Mass over the body of St. Peter." During his reign a platform was built to raise the *presbytery* within the apse and the main altar was placed on it, directly above the top of the tomb. At the same time, by lowering the original pavement of the apse, a crypt was inserted beneath the platform. It was semi-circular in plan, with a central passage leading from the wall of the apse to the back of the shrine, and became known as the Covered Confessio. At the beginning of the seventeenth century, the central passage was rebuilt into a chapel called the Cappella Clementina.

Together, the platform and altar concealed all of the shrine from view except for the niche in its east front, flanked by the stairs which led up to the presbytery. However, only a small section of the niche remained visible below the altar and so another recess had to be cut into the tomb. This was deeper, though more narrow and not as tall as the one it replaced, and was decorated by a mosaic of Our Lord that was protected by a grille of gilded bronze. It was called the Niche of the Pallia because of the age-old practice of placing vestments, the *pallia*, in a deep shaft within the floor of the shrine before being sent, by the Pope, to all newly consecrated metropolitans (archbishops). They signify that the metropolitans share the Pontiff's supreme pastoral power.

With the alteration of the apse and shrine, the baldacchino which Emperor Constantine had erected was dismantled. Its four columns and the two others of the same set, which had stood against the shoulders of the apse, were rearranged to form a two-part screen before the platform, three to the left, and three to the right of the Niche of the Pallia. A new canopy, of silver, was then erected on the presbytery over the tomb.

In the eighth century the exarch of Ravenna, governor of Italy, presented Pope Gregory III (731-741) with six marble columns of the same spiral shape and carved details as those from Constantine. These were positioned in the transept as an outer screen in front of the first six columns. They carried a silver *architrave* engraved with the images of the Saviour and the Apostles, and the Mother of God with the Holy Virgins.

Gregory the Great's silver baldacchino remained over the shrine for about two hundred years until Pope Leo III (795-816) sent it to the church of Santa Maria Maggiore. He had another silver one constructed in its place, and before it, on Christmas Day A.D. 800, crowned Charlemagne Emperor of the Holy Roman Empire.

27

During the terrible Sack of Rome in 846, the Saracens raided St. Peter's, which they "invaded and occupied . . . committing unspeakable iniquities." Within a week the infidels had stripped the basilica of all its valuables, including the altar, and violated the tomb beneath in search of jewels and gold.

Pope Leo IV (847-855) had the church repaired, restored the damaged frescoes and mosaics, and somehow managed to replace most of its stolen decorations with new ornaments. Then, to protect St. Peter's from future attacks, he had a high wall built around Vatican Hill, 10,800 feet in circumference, which enclosed an area not much smaller than today's Vatican City. The great wall, with its two fortified towers, was constructed by the citizens of Rome over a period of four years and was blessed by the Pope in 852.

Despite continued maintenance after Leo IV's restoration, St. Peter's basilica began to show serious signs of its advanced age. Pope Gregory VI (1045-1046) had to plead for funds to make structural repairs on the church which was at that time, dating from the year of its consecration, 719 years old. Later popes patched and mended the building in their efforts to strengthen its leaning walls. Pope Benedict XI (1303-1304) alone spent the equivalent of $500,000 on it.

But Clement V (1305-1314), who followed Benedict as Pontiff, moved the papal court to Avignon, France, and old St. Peter's was neglected until Pope Gregory XI (1370-1378) returned to Rome in 1377. The basilica had deteriorated alarmingly by then, yet little was done to recondition it during the years of the Great Schism, from 1378 to 1417, when the Church was divided against itself. Pope Martin V (1417-1431), who healed the breach, gave the aged edifice its first major repairs in

Filarete's bronze doors

over a hundred years. He also began the reconstruction of Rome—an undertaking that continued on until almost the end of the sixteenth century.

After the renovation of St. Peter's, Martin V's successor, Eugene IV (1431-1447), commissioned Filarete to design and cast two tremendous bronze doors for the main entrance of the church. These are the doors which now hang in the center portal of the present basilica. Their six panels, executed in relief, depict: Our Saviour Enthroned, Our Lady Enthroned, St. Paul with the Sword, St. Peter giving the Keys to Eugene IV, the Beheading of St. Paul, and the Crucifixion of St. Peter. Small scenes from Roman history and classical mythology separate the six panels, which are surrounded by a richly decorated, intricately detailed border of a rhythmic *rinceau* design. Filarete worked on the doors twelve years before they were completed and installed in old St. Peter's in 1445.

Only a few years later, the ancient basilica was once again in an extremely poor condition. Its weakened clerestory walls, measured by architect Leon Alberti, had bulged out six-and-a-half feet from their original vertical position, and seemed ready to collapse.

Pope Nicholas V (1447-1455) decided to replace rather than restore the tottering structure. He then appointed Alberti and Bernardo Rossellino to collaborate on a design for the new church, and they envisioned it in the form of a Latin cross. It was to be 640 feet long and 320 feet wide across the transepts, with a dome over the crossing to rise 220 feet above the ground. The plan received the approval of the Pope and work was started on the west apse in 1454. Little was accomplished, however, for the following year Nicholas V died and construction was suspended.

Michelangelo's *Pietà*

Nine years later, Pope Paul II (1464-1471) resumed the work, saw that the half-finished foundations of the new apse were completed and its walls built. But his successor, Sixtus IV (1471-1484), did not advance the rebuilding. Instead, he had the interior of the basilica redecorated, placed a new baldacchino with columns of porphyry over the main altar, and concentrated on the construction of another building in the Vatican, the Sistine Chapel, which he consecrated in 1483. More than twenty years passed before the rebuilding of St. Peter's began in earnest.

Julius II, the Founder

Although the enormous task of erecting a great new basilica finally got underway during the reign of Pope Julius II (1503-1513), promoting the project had not been his first intention.

Donato Bramante, one of the foremost architects of his time, had been engaged by Pope Alexander VI (1492-1503) to remodel and unify the complex of buildings that comprised the Vatican Palace. He was still engrossed with the task when Julius II was elected to the pontifical throne. Pope Julius, quite satisfied with the work already done on the Court of San Damaso and the Belvedere, retained Bramante to continue his program of beautifying the Vatican, but that, for the time being, was the extent of Bramante's responsibilities.

Shortly afterwards, however, during an inspection of the old basilica, the Pope discovered Michelangelo's beautiful *Pietà* which was then in the circular south-side Chapel of St. Petronilla. This is the internationally known marble masterpiece which represents the grieving Madonna with the lifeless body of Christ lying across her knees. It had been completed by Michelangelo in 1499, at the age of twenty-four. The Pope was impressed by the pathos and perfection of the statue and sensed the genius of its creator. He summoned Michelangelo to Rome in 1505, and in March of that year, commissioned the gifted sculptor to carve him a magnificent tomb.

Michelangelo designed a memorial for Julius II that was not only magnificent, but colossal as well. It was to be four-sided, triple-tiered, and adorned with thirty-eight life-sized statues; and was so big—18 feet high and 12 feet wide—that it took him six months to select enough marble from the quarries at Carrara.

During Michelangelo's absence, the Pope faced the problem of housing his newly proposed tomb. He had wanted it to stand in the old basilica, but found that the available space was too small for its accommodation. Bramante, Fra Giocondo and Giuliano da Sangallo were consulted. They proposed to finish the apse begun by Nicholas V, then demolish the choir and connect the enlarged unit to the rest of the church. Pope Julius considered their recommendation inadequate

Bramante's plan

and promptly resolved to build a new St. Peter's that would, in his words, "embody the greatness of the present and the future . . . [and] surpass all other churches in the universe." In October he organized a competition among a number of notable architects. From the designs submitted—still kept in the Uffizi Gallery in Florence—the one drawn by Bramante was chosen.

Bramante's plan for St. Peter's was a spacious Greek cross, with four arms of equal length which ended in semi-circular apses. The cross shape was modified to an almost square outline by sacristies placed in the spaces between the arms that were also Greek-cross forms, roofed by small domes. An *ambulatory* or gallery ran around the south, west, and north sides, and a tall tower rose up at each of the four corners. If the church had been completed according to this plan, it would have covered a total surface area of 28,700 square yards, or 11,350 square yards more than the space occupied by the present basilica.

The dominating feature of Bramante's design was a great central dome. He had been inspired by the Pantheon in Rome and had used its saucer-shaped dome as a model. Like its ancient Roman archetype, Bramante's dome was to be of solid masonry, with rows of stepped buttressing circling its base. Its internal diameter would have been about 142 feet—equal to the Pantheon's.

Bramante's façade (west end)

33

But the once-pagan temple was a simple circular building. Its dome, built upon a continuous wall, 20 feet thick, roofed the entire structure except for the front portico and vestibule. In contrast, Bramante's plan was complex, for the central position of his dome required supports twice as high as those of the Pantheon to be exteriorly impressive. He proposed to set the dome on a high drum upheld by four giant-sized piers. He also planned to have an outer *peristyle*, a range of columns around the drum, and a lantern with cross surmounting the dome. The over-all height would have reached 300 feet, while the Pantheon was just 147 feet high.

When Michelangelo returned from Carrara, in the fall of 1505, he directed all his energy to Julius II's tomb. The Pope, then preoccupied with Bramante and the plans for the new basilica, showed little interest in the sculptor's project. He did, however, find time to reconsider the design for his monument and ordered the artist to reduce its size. One cannot imagine Michelangelo accepting the command without protest, for he was quick-tempered and often difficult to deal with. Adding insult to injury, the day before the laying of the cornerstone of St. Peter's, the Pope told him to suspend work on the tomb temporarily. Disappointed and angry, Michelangelo abruptly packed his belongings and sped on horseback to the Florentine Republic. Although Julius II made several attempts to coax him back, Michelangelo defiantly stayed in Florence for two years. His reconciliation with the Pope came in 1508, at which time he reluctantly agreed to paint a series of frescoes on the immense ceiling of the Sistine Chapel.

On April 18, 1506, Julius II, attended by two cardinals and two masons, climbed down into an excavation twenty-five feet deep where he deposited an urn containing commemorative coins and medals. Over the urn he set a block of marble "four palms wide, two broad, and three fingers thick," which he blessed with holy water. This was the foundation stone of the Pier of St. Veronica; its inscription named Pope Julius II the Founder, and gave the date and reason for rebuilding —the ruinous condition of the ancient edifice. The foundation stones of the other central piers, dedicated to Sts. Helena, Andrew, and Longinus, were laid in 1507.

Under Bramante's direction, no fewer than 2,500 laborers were employed on the construction. They made rapid progress and by 1510 all four colossal piers had been completed and, within another year, their *pendentives* and the great coffered arches that span them were in place. Once built, this unit permanently established the dimensions of the huge central crossing and even though many changes were made by later architects, it remained the nucleus of the basilica.

At the beginning of the rebuilding, Bramante designed a Doric chapel or altar-house to protect the shrine. It was large enough to shelter the apse of the old church and all of the raised platform of the presbytery, including the inner screen of Constantine's spiral columns. Begun in 1507, completed about 1524, the stone chapel remained standing in the center of the crossing until 1592 when it was

Bramante's Doric chapel

torn down to make way for the new high altar.

Pope Julius died in February, 1513. His tomb, with its celebrated central figure of Moses, was never quite finished. It was much smaller than originally designed, and because of many interruptions, had taken much longer to execute than Michelangelo intended. In 1545 the monument was placed, not in St. Peter's as Julius had planned, but in the Church of San Pietro in Vincoli in Rome.

Bramante's death occurred in 1514. By then the west apse, begun by Alberti and Rossellino in 1454, had been redesigned by Bramante and completed, although it would be rebuilt and enlarged more than a half-century later. Work was also in progress on two side chapels and the buttressing piers of the north and south arms of the cross.

Michelangelo's *Moses*

Bramante's Successors

For a few months following the death of Bramante, Giuliano da Sangallo and Fra Giocondo supervised the construction of the new St. Peter's. Sangallo worked on a design for the east portico and its two flanking towers; Fra Giocondo on the plans for a sacristy next to the west apse. However, both men were old and ailing, and in August, 1514, Pope Leo X (1513-1521) delegated a prominent young artist, Raphael, to the post of chief architect of St. Peter's. This appointment was in accordance with the last wishes of Bramante, Raphael's devoted uncle.

Earlier, in 1508, Raphael had been commissioned to decorate the Stanze, the State Apartments of the Vatican Palace, with a series of paintings. He executed the work over a period of three years, and during that time, having been closely associated with Bramante, acquired a knowledge of the elements of architecture. Leo X was aware of Raphael's limited experience and retained Fra Giocondo and Sangallo as his assistants, but the former died in 1515, the latter in 1516.

36

Raphael's façade

Detail drawing by Raphael

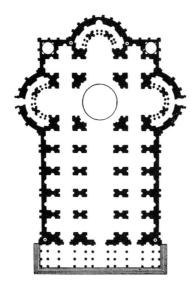

Raphael's plan

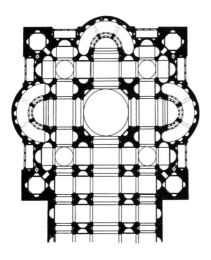

Peruzzi's plan

Raphael's design for St. Peter's altered Bramante's Greek-cross plan to a Latin cross. Yet he accomplished not much more than the strengthening of the crossing piers before his untimely death in 1520 at the age of thirty-seven. In his role as director-of-the-works, Raphael had always been agreeable and accommodating. Compliantly, but unwisely, he allowed masons to leave gaps in the foundations so that workmen could have convenient storage space for their lunches, firewood, and tools. Several years later the faulty sections began to fracture and crumble from the strain of the weighty structure above and had to be rebuilt without hollows.

Baldassare Peruzzi succeeded Raphael and reverted to a Greek-cross plan. But building funds were low and construction proceeded at a snail's pace. The major advancement during Peruzzi's sixteen years of service was on the south side of the basilica where the barrel vaults, which connect the buttressing piers to the piers of the crossing, were completed, and coffered with decorative recessed panels. At the same time, the side walls of the south arm were brought to their full height and the semi-circular outer wall of its terminal apse was partially built.

The Sack of Rome in 1527, in which almost 12,000 people were slain, and all but one-third of the dwellings in the city were demolished, lasted from May to October. During those months the marauding Spanish forces—abetted by German and Italian mercenaries—used the Vatican *loggias* as their headquarters, stabled their horses in the Sistine Chapel, and swarmed over Rome looting everywhere, terrorizing the populace with violent acts of torture and murder. They thoroughly plundered St. Peter's, broke into the shrine, desecrated sacred objects, and in their vandalism

Above: Sack of Rome. Below: Central piers and arches.

deliberately damaged everything of value that could not be carried away. Work
on the basilica, which ceased at the onset of the devastating attack, was not resumed until the pontificate of Paul III (1534-1549). By then the tops of the piers
and arches built by Bramante had sprouted a lush growth of grass and bushy
weeds.

When Peruzzi died in 1536, Antonio da Sangallo the Younger was appointed
chief architect. He was the nephew of Giuliano da Sangallo and had been employed at St. Peter's from 1506 onward, beginning as a carpenter, later advancing
to the rank of assistant architect.

Antonio elaborated on Peruzzi's design by adding a large front vestibule flanked by two lofty bell towers. In effect he created a compromise between the previous Latin- and Greek-cross plans, for the lengthened vestibule had the appearance of a short, semi-nave projecting from the eastern arm. His other proposals included: construction of minor domes over the four corners of the church, closing off the ambulatories around the terminal apses, and walling up the niches in the crossing piers. He designed the central dome as a single shell, 42 feet thick at its base, 17 feet thick at its top, with a coffered inner surface. Its exterior, ribbed on the upper half, was to be girded by two colonnades from the mid-section down.

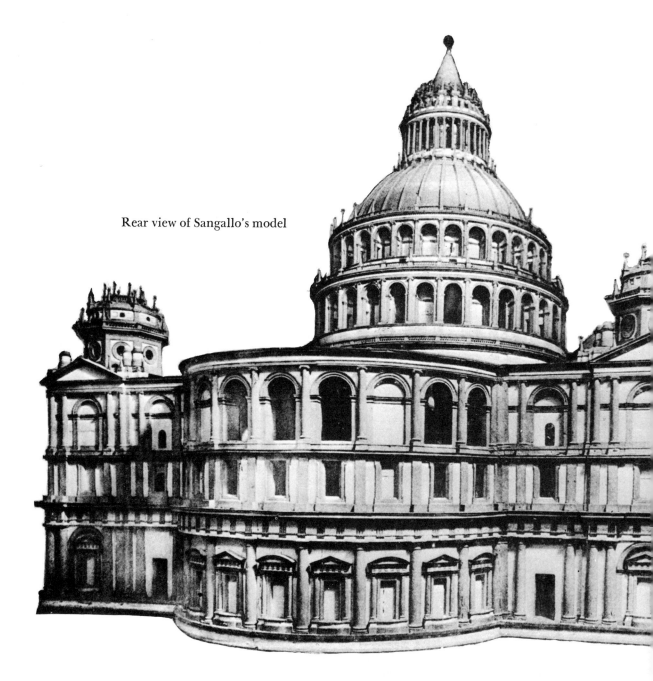

Rear view of Sangallo's model

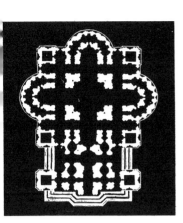

Sangallo's plan

Front view of Sangallo's model

Over a period of seven years, Sangallo worked on a large, finely detailed model of his conception of St. Peter's which was later criticized as being too ambitious, overly ornate, and a reversion to the Latin-cross plan. Made of wood, at a cost of 4,000 Italian crowns, it is still preserved in the Museo Petriano of the Vatican.

So many differences arose between Sangallo and his associates that the architect requested his own dismissal and Pope Paul III selected Giuliano Romano to take his place as director. When both Romano and Sangallo died in 1546, the Pope called on Michelangelo to continue the task of rebuilding.

41

Painting by Passignani

Michelangelo

In 1546, Michelangelo, at the age of seventy-one, was already occupied with the painting of two frescoes in the Pauline Chapel of the Vatican Palace. These great works, finished in 1550, were then far from complete and he had to be persuaded to take on the added responsibilities of chief architect of St. Peter's. When the artist at last agreed to direct the construction, it was only on condition that he be allowed to dedicate his labor for the love of God, St. Peter, and Our Saviour's Mother. He assumed full charge in 1547 and throughout the remainder of his life, though plagued by hostile rivals, supervised the undertaking wholeheartedly, and almost single handed, without personal remuneration.

Pope Paul's official letter gave Michelangelo plenary power—absolute and full authority—to manage the operations as he saw fit. He had the right to make any alterations necessary to conform with his plans, even if it involved destruction of parts already completed, and although he was to control large funds, he was not under obligation to keep formal records of the expenditures.

Michelangelo set aside all of Sangallo's drawings and plans. Within two weeks he produced a new design and a clay model to illustrate his proposed changes, and soon afterwards constructed a larger, wooden scale-model of the basilica. Both disappeared long ago, but a painting by Passignani, done in 1620, depicts Michelangelo showing the wooden model to the Pope. It was flat-roofed and lacking a façade, with a dome and side cupolas that are believed to have been added years later by Della Porta.

42

Michelangelo's model of dome

43

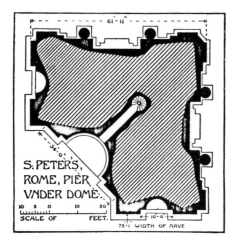

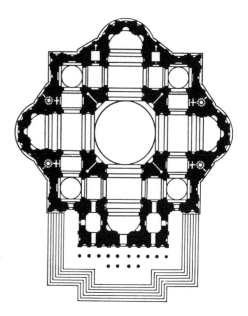

Cross-section of central pier

Michelangelo's plan

Michelangelo's design, enthusiastically approved by Paul III, was a return to the Greek-cross plan of Bramante. However, he modified the original version considerably and actually retained only the cross formation and the central dome from Bramante's scheme. He eliminated Sangallo's vestibule with its bell towers, the ambulatories around the semi-circular apses, and reduced the number of chapels and niches. He decreased the size of the four corner sacristies by altering their Greek crosses to plainer domed sections, and joined them to the main arms with double barrel vaults. The basilica on plan was a cross superimposed upon a huge square, more compact, of smaller dimensions than before, but better organized, with formerly isolated parts unified into a perfectly connected aggregate. The interior was to be 450 feet long and 450 feet wide across the transepts, with all details scaled to heroic proportions in harmony with the colossal exterior. For the entrance at the end of the eastern arm, Michelangelo proposed a pedimented portico of fourteen free-standing columns, each almost 100 feet high and seven feet in diameter.

His dome, the most daring and most majestic ever conceived, followed the structural system of multiple shells exemplified by Brunelleschi in the dome of Santa Maria del Fiore at Florence (1420-1434). Though then only tentatively drawn, it would be much higher, lighter, and far more graceful than the single-shell domes intended by Bramante and Sangallo.

Raphael, Peruzzi, and Sangallo had, in turn, strengthened the central piers, yet they were still considered shaky. Michelangelo immediately reinforced all four by

44

having deep holes dug beneath their foundations which were filled in with masonry. In August of 1547 a windlass, ramps, and scaffolding were erected and work was begun on the interior cornice of the base of the drum.

During the next year the walls of the north arm were completed and the outer wall of the south ambulatory was torn down. Sangallo's admirers, rival architects, and many papal deputies protested the demolition in vain and from then on never ceased their criticism. They resented Michelangelo's secrecy about the plans, the changes he made without consulting anyone, and conspired to have him discharged by slandering his character. In spite of the persistent opposition and vicious attempts to discredit him, Paul III and his successors maintained their confidence in Michelangelo and continued to support him.

By 1557, work on the drum had progressed more than halfway toward completion. Michelangelo was in his tenth year as chief architect, but had not yet come to a definite decision on the proportion and profile of the dome. His friends, Bandini and Cardinal Rodolfo Pio, were concerned because the body of the church was still "without a head." They worried that Michelangelo might die without leaving any specifications to complete the dome and pressed him to finalize his designs and construct a model. Michelangelo complied and in July sculptured a small dome of clay which he supplemented with a few detail sketches. Working from these, Messer Giovanni Franzese constructed a large wooden scale-model which he finished in late 1561. It was one-fifteenth the size of the actual dome, and made with particular care for accuracy so that it could be closely followed by the builders.

View of piers and arches, north side

The dome model, which still stands in the Museo Petriano, has a cutaway section that exposes three shells, while the dome, as executed, has only two. For a long time this fact led authorities to believe that Michelangelo first planned a triple-shelled dome and afterward decided to eliminate the inner, hemispherical shell. Eventually differences in craftsmanship were noted and the model was given more careful examination. About 1932 it was concluded that, although Michelangelo had made changes in the model after its completion, the outer shell is the work of Della Porta, probably done in 1578. This would account for the almost identical contours and details of the actual dome and the model.

In 1560, a subordinate complained to the Pope that serious mistakes were being made because Michelangelo, then eighty-five, was too old and no longer mentally or physically fit to direct the work. Michelangelo attempted to resign, but Pius IV (1559-1565) refused to accept his petition. Instead, the Pope had an impartial expert examine the construction to find the alleged errors, and fired the meddling assistant when his charges were proved to be false. Then Pius sent the elderly architect a decree which reaffirmed Michelangelo's plenary power, and emphatically forbade any alteration of his plans.

Despite a stroke, suffered in 1561, Michelangelo proved his mind was as alert as ever by winning a competition for the design of a church, Santa Maria degli Angeli, which Pope Pius proposed to build in the Vatican. By 1563, however, his physical debility had become a great hindrance. He had to be lifted on and off his horse, and required the assistance of Vignola and Pirro Ligorio when he was no longer able to climb the high scaffolding to inspect the building. Toward the end of that year his responsibilities were greatly eased with the appointment of F. de Cortona as supervising architect. Michelangelo died a few months later, on February 18, 1564, after seventeen years of service under no fewer than five popes.

The huge drum, 137½ feet in diameter and over 600 feet in circumference, was then complete except for a section of its entablature on the western half. It is pierced by sixteen pedimented windows, 20 feet high, and ringed by a peristyle of coupled Corinthian columns, 50 feet tall, which represent the ends of the masses of buttressing that radiate out from the wall of the drum. The columns stand upon a circular pedestal that rests on an octagonal base which is level with the roof top and directly supported by the piers and pendentives of the crossing.

Michelangelo had planned on having graceful scroll-shaped ornaments, inverted *consoles*, set above the peristyle on the sixteen ledges formed by the buttresses. He designed them to provide an intergradation or "transition" between the drum and the curve of the dome, and wanted them to be accentuated by monumental statues of saints. Unfortunately they were omitted when the dome was finally built, as was a balustrade he proposed for the top of the drum's entablature.

Fresco showing atrium façade and almost completed drum (1571-72)

Side cupola of St. Peter's

Michelangelo's Successors

Immediately following the death of Michelangelo, Pius IV appointed Ligorio chief architect, with Vignola as his associate. Ligorio, who built the Casino, a little summer house in the Vatican gardens, had been one of the factionists in dispute with Michelangelo. He could not resist the temptation to revise the plans and was discharged by the next pope, Pius V (1566-1572). Vignola then received the post and held it for six years, from 1567 until his death in 1573. He completed the entablature of the drum, the vaulting of the north apse, and started the construction of a huge domed chapel on the northeast corner, according to the plans left by Michelangelo.

Pope Gregory XIII (1572-1585) succeeded Pius V, and after Vignola died, named Giacomo della Porta chief architect, with Domenico Fontana as his assistant. The Pontiff's primary interest was the completion of the northeast chapel and the construction of another directly opposite on the southeast corner; both the same size, they are the two largest in St. Peter's. The first one, finished in 1578 and dedicated to Our Lady of Help, later became known as the Gregorian Chapel; the second, begun in 1579 and opened in 1600, is the Clementine Chapel. Although their twin cupolas have often been credited to Vignola, they were redesigned and rebuilt by Della Porta. About 1580, the west apse was rebuilt and enlarged in conformation with the north and south arms, and by 1585, the year Gregory XIII died, its vaulting was under construction.

50

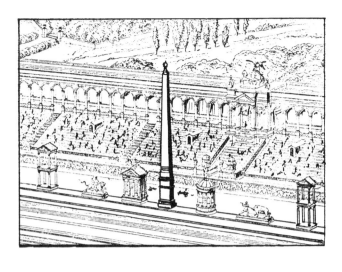

Top: Obelisk as it stood in Nero's Circus. Bottom: Obelisk as it appeared at north side of old basilica. Right: Obelisk on its present site.

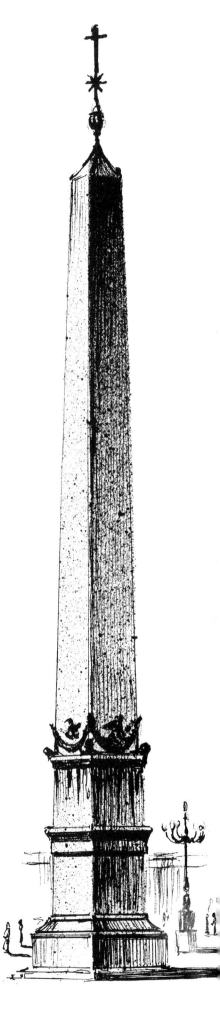

It was during the reign of Sixtus V (1585-1590) that the great central dome was built, but work on that long-delayed project did not begin until almost two years after the red granite obelisk that is associated with the execution of St. Peter was erected in the Piazza di San Pietro. The huge monolith, 82 feet tall and weighing an estimated 320 tons, had been brought to Rome from Heliopolis, Egypt, by Emperor Caligula (A.D. 37-41) who had it set up in a stadium later known as the Circus of Nero. For centuries it stood close by the south wall of the basilica marking what was believed to be the buried

Fresco depicting obelisk en route to the piazza

spina, the central divider, of the arena where St. Peter had been crucified and martyred.

Sixtus V had not been the first pope to think of moving it to a more prominent place. Over 130 years earlier, Nicholas V had expressed the same idea to his architect, Alberti, as they made plans for the rebuilding of St. Peter's. Some years later Alberti, working under Paul II, prepared a carefully detailed scheme for its removal to the piazza, but the Pope died before anything could be done. Under Julius II, Bramante considered making the Egyptian stone a focal point in front of the church and first planned to have the basilica face south, toward the obelisk.

Since the proposal would have necessitated moving the tomb, Pope Julius rejected it—the church would have to face east, and Bramante could do what he pleased with the obelisk. Apparently Bramante did not give the matter another thought, nor did anyone else for the next eighty years until Sixtus V decided to take action.

Soon after his election in 1585, Pope Sixtus announced his intention to move the great stone to the center of the piazza and invited engineers to compete for the contract. Over one hundred plans were submitted, and that of Domenico Fontana was selected, though it still had to be proved practicable.

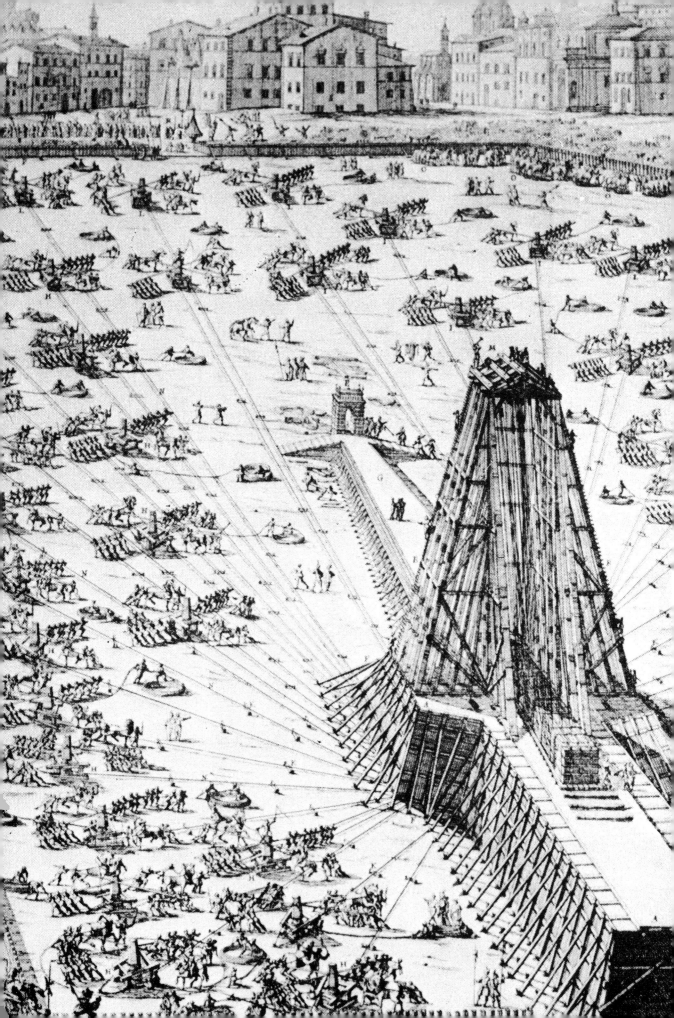

Old engraving showing erection of the obelisk

In the fall of that year Fontana convinced the Pope that he could lift the obelisk off its ancient base and re-erect it, undamaged, by building a large wooden model on the piazza with which he demonstrated his ability and method. Preparations for the transfer began at once and were completed the following spring. Fontana had a massive towering crane of heavy oak beams constructed around the obelisk, and a wooden roadway laid from its site to its destination over a quarter-mile away. Then the solid granite shaft was crated in boards, bound with iron bands, and rigged with forty thick hemp lines, each 350 feet long, which were attached to as many windlasses. When all was ready, on April 25, 1586, with the power of 800 laborers and 200 horses, the obelisk was successfully pulled up from its foundation and gently lowered down onto a long flatcar for the short but slow journey to its permanent location. Afterward the crane was dismantled and hauled piece by piece to the piazza where it was set up again for the raising of the huge stone to its new base. The momentous occasion took place on September 10, and as a reward for his accomplishment, Fontana was made a Knight of the Golden Spur and given a pension of 2,000 crowns. The total height of the obelisk with its base and bronze cross, which has a piece of the True Cross inside, is 132 feet.

55

Fresco (1588-90) showing obelisk in center of Piazza di San Pierto

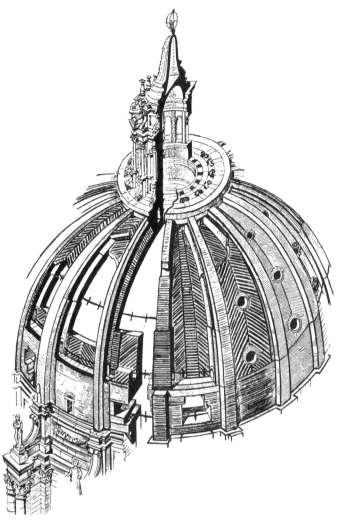

Diagram of dome's construction

By the spring of 1588 the vaulting of the west apse had been completed, and a few months later, in July, work was started on the great central dome. While most authorities agreed that its construction would take at least ten years, Sixtus V was determined to have the dome finished far sooner. He gave Della Porta and Fontana a limit of two and a half years, yet allowed them such ample funds that they were able to employ 800 masons and laborers on the site. With crews working day and night shifts, construction went on continuously, interrupted only for observances of the Sabbath.

On May 14, 1590, the last stone was put in place and Sixtus V offered a Solemn Mass of Thanksgiving in the basilica. The Pope was satisfied, for he had initiated the construction of the dome, and seen it completed in the astonishingly short period of twenty-two months—twenty-six years after the death of its designer.

Della Porta altered the dome's contour and enhanced its soaring aspect by making it 20 feet higher and more pointed than Michelangelo planned—a change that had been previously approved by Sixtus V in 1586. As executed, the dome's two shells are of brick set in a herringbone pattern. Its skeletal structure consists of

59

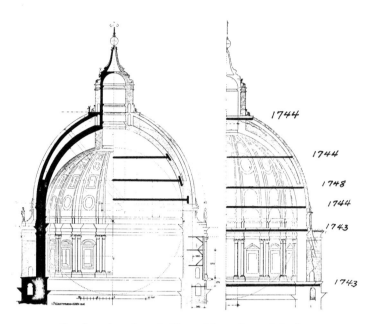

1744
1744
1748
1744
1743
1743

Section showing shells and location of chains

sixteen well defined stone ribs which extend through both shells and, though they are all of uniform width, appear to taper as they stretch up from the solid wall of the dome's lower quarter, to the base of the lantern at its crown. However, because the shells are not concentric, the ribs gradually increase in depth as they rise, and are almost twice as thick at the top as they are at the base of the dome. Three rows of windows admit light to the space between the shells, and narrow stairs cut into the *extrados*, the upper curved surface or back, of the inner hemisphere provide passages to the lantern 269 steps above.

As it was being built, three cincture chains were set into the dome to prevent it from spreading: two embedded in the solid mass of brick at its springing, where the curve begins, and another midway to the summit. Yet, over a century and a half later, when cracks and fissures appeared, an examination disclosed that the ribs of the dome had begun to buckle outward because of the tremendous weight of the lantern, and the drum, in turn, showed a slight expansion at its top. Engineers advised the Pope, Benedict XIV (1740-1758), to have chains placed around the base and top of the drum and three more around the dome, because it was impossible to determine whether or not the original ones had given way. The five chains were inserted within the structure between 1743 and 1744 under the direction of architect Vanvitelli. A sixth chain was added in 1748, and since then the dome has remained sound.

Sixtus V died three months after the dome's completion. Although his successors, Urban VII, Gregory XIV and Innocent IX, were all short-lived, construction

60

Cross-section of lantern

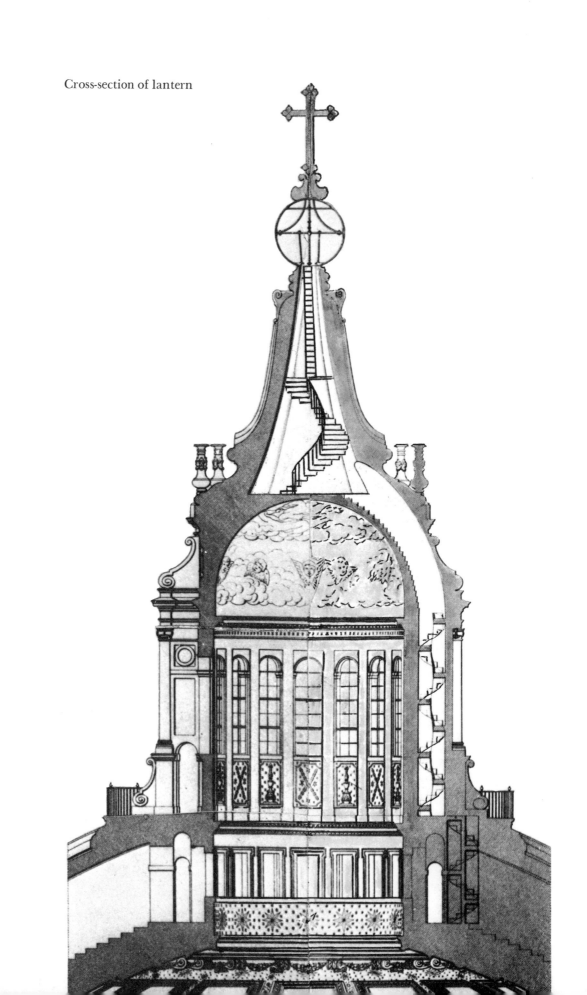

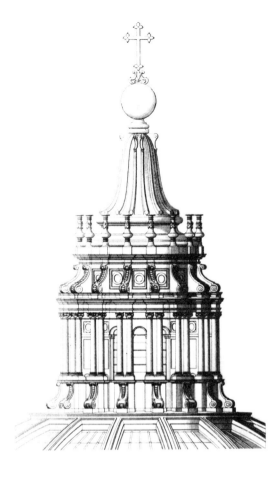

Elevation of lantern. Right: Section showing spiral staircase in lantern's wall.

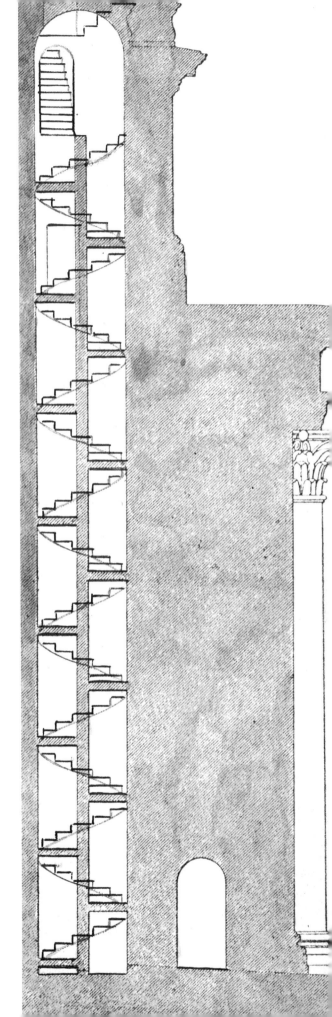

went on uninterrupted. The graceful stone lantern with its paired columns, inverted consoles, and delicate, concave spire that crowns the dome was built under Della Porta and Fontana, and finished during the reign of Pope Clement VIII (1592-1605). Its great copper ball and cross, rising 452 feet above the pavement of the basilica, was made in the papal foundry and surmounted to the lantern on November 18, 1593. Ascent to the ball is provided by a spiral staircase in the lantern's wall which gives access to a range of steps above the vault. A second spiral staircase, in the spire, leads to a perpendicular iron ladder that extends into the ball, eight feet in diameter, where there is standing room for as many as sixteen people.

Detail: Angel head of dome mosaics

Within Clement VIII's pontificate the Clementine Chapel on the south side of St. Peter's was finished, and the central passage of the crypt was remodeled by Della Porta into the Cappella Clementina. Both were dedicated in 1600. Pope Clement commissioned Provenzale to embellish the vaulting of the Clementine Chapel with mosaics of the Doctors of the Church; Della Porta, for the mosaics of the Cappella Clementina; and engaged other well-known artists to paint several huge altarpieces which were later reproduced in mosaic. In 1598, he employed Giuseppe Cesari, also known as the Cavalier D'Arpino, to design the spectacular mosaics which decorate the sixteen rib-divided sections of the dome's vast interior and the vault of the lantern.

Cesari and a crew of assistants executed a large part of the masterpiece during Pope Clement's lifetime, but, because the project was so enormous, the work was not completed until 1612. It consists of beautiful, majestic representations of Christ the Saviour, His Mother Mary, the Apostles, angels, saints and popes, which are resplendent with gold and lustrous gradations of white, blue, red and purple. Through the *oculus* at the top of the dome can be seen the great image of God in heavenly atmosphere, bestowing His blessing upon mankind. An inscription round the oculus informs the viewer that the dome was built for the glory of St. Peter by Sixtus V. Circling the lower rim, on a broad band of gold mosaic, is a second inscription in dark blue letters, five feet high: TU ES PETRUS ET SUPER HANC PETRAM AEDIFICABO MEAM ET TIBI DABO CLAVES REGNI COELORUM. (Thou art Peter, and upon this rock I will build my church, and I will give unto thee the keys of the Kingdom of Heaven. Matt. 16: 18-19.)

65

S. Maria

S. Petri

S. Anna

P. Angelica

PLATEA·S·PETRI

Campo·Sancto

Cesis

S. Spirito

Guardia de cavalli leggieri

P. de cavalli·leg·

Although Fontana out-lived Della Porta by three years, when the latter died in 1604, Carlo Maderna, Fontana's nephew, was appointed to the post of chief architect. By then the massive outer walls of St. Peter's had been completed almost to the boundary line across the east arm, where—according to Michelangelo's Greek-cross plan—the façade and columned portico were to be built. At this time about one-quarter of Constantine's ancient basilica was still standing: part of the nave, all of the front, the porch, and the atrium before it. These were destined to be demolished, with the graves and monuments of popes buried there transferred to the crypts beneath the new St. Peter's. But a sizable portion of ground occupied by the old church, hallowed by centuries of worship, extended beyond the limits of Michelangelo's design. This fact, coupled with the need for more adequate space to accommodate great crowds of worshipers attending special celebrations, raised the question of whether or not to lengthen the nave and cover the remainder of the old churchsite. A decision was still pending when Pope Clement's death occurred in March, 1605. His immediate successor, Leo XI, had no opportunity to consider the question, for his reign lasted only twenty-six days.

Paul V (1605-1621), elected Pontiff in May, confirmed Carlo Maderna's appointment as chief architect and spent the next few months pondering the problem of construction with his cardinals. In September the choice was made to extend the eastern arm by 200 feet and convert the basilica from Greek-cross to Latin-cross form. The Papal Building Commission, delegated to invite architects to submit designs for the addition, received nine proposals. Maderna's plan for a nave of three bays, which continued Michelangelo's system of arches, coffered barrel vaults, and colossal Corinthian pilasters, was selected.

Early in 1606 the Pope assigned a second commission to supervise the opening of graves and dismantling of altars and monuments for consignment to the crypts, as demolition of the remaining portion of the old basilica began. In 1607, Maderna's plan was given a final approval and the cornerstone of the nave was laid; a year later, that of the massive façade and portico.

Left: Engraving of 1593

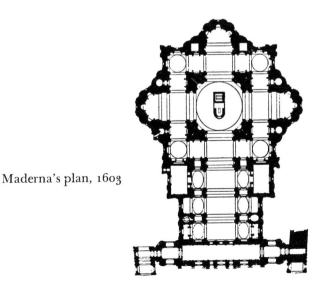

Maderna's plan, 1603

Elevation drawing of Maderna's façade

An army of 1,000 workmen, directed by Maderna and his assistants, toiled night and day on orders of Paul V to speed the construction. By 1612, the great nave, façade, and pedimented portico, which unavoidably obscured a close-up view of all but the top of the central dome, were externally complete.

It was also in 1612 that Maderna built the U-shaped Open Confessio in front of the High Altar and designed, in accordance with Paul V's wishes, twin fountains to be erected on either side of the obelisk in the Piazza di San Pietro, and bell towers to flank the façade. The first fountain, on the right, was built in 1613, yet its mate was not constructed until sixty years later, during the reign of Pope Clement X (1670-1676). Work on the two bell towers started in 1613, but ceased with the death of Pope Paul in 1621 when only the substructures were finished.

70

In 1614, the nave vault was raised—slightly higher than Sangallo's vaulting with which it connects; the ancient bronze statue of St. Peter was installed at the south side of the pier of St. Longinus; and the monumental statues, 19 feet tall, of the Saviour and the Apostles, which stand atop the façade, were unveiled. The basilica was then opened to the public, although the front steps were not constructed until 1617. That year, ancient statues of St. Peter and St. Paul were positioned at the sides of the stairs, but these were replaced by the present ones during the reign of Pope Pius IX (1846-1878).

The interior of the portico, its ceiling richly decorated with portrayals of the Acts of the Apostles, scenes from the lives of martyred popes, and elegant stucco work designed by Maderna, was completed in 1619. Soon after, in 1620, Filarete's great bronze doors that had been salvaged from old St. Peter's and restored, were hung in the central entrance, and the Holy Door, on the extreme right or north side, was built and sealed. The thirty statues of seated popes placed over the cornice were executed by the sculptors Valsoldo and Bonvicino; the latter was also responsible for the large relief of *Christ Handing Over the Keys to St. Peter* which is beneath the Balcony of Benediction, above the central, outer doorway.

When Paul V died, the basilica was complete, but its impressive interior, except for the dome and portico, was mostly unadorned. Under Gregory XV (1621-1623), Maderna directed the task of surfacing sections of the walls and pavement with marble and continued this work until his death in 1629.

Statues atop façade of St. Peter's   Opposite: Ancient bronze statue of St. Peter

Bernini

In 1624, Pope Urban VIII (1623-1644) commissioned the foremost sculptor of the day, young Giovanni Lorenzo Bernini, to build a great baldacchino over the High Altar above the Tomb of St. Peter. Bernini, a child prodigy, the son of a well-known Florentine sculptor, had been introduced to the papal court at the age of ten and achieved international fame when only eighteen with his marble group, *Apollo and Daphne*. He was a master of the spiritually vibrant, emotion-stirring Baroque style, a favored genius highly esteemed by Urban VIII and later popes, as well as by contemporary artists.

Bernini was twenty-five when he entered the service of the Pope and spent the remaining fifty-six years of his life almost exclusively engaged with the execution of ecclesiastical art and architecture and the lavish, remarkable embellishment of St. Peter's. Besides completing much of the basilica's interior decorations, Bernini culminated his career with the mighty elliptical colonnades of the Piazza di San Pietro and gave St. Peter's the grandest approach of any church in the world.

Bernini began work on the magnificent bronze and gilt baldacchino in July, 1624, and was occupied for three years preparing models and personally supervising the casting of the columns. They were unveiled in June, 1627, seven months after Pope Urban consecrated the basilica. Bernini perfected his designs for the canopy and its ornamental details, but was forced to rely on others for their execution when he succeeded Maderna as chief architect in 1629 and was assigned to draw plans for the decoration of the dome pillars.

Bronze and gilt column of baldacchino

Bernini's early projects for baldacchino

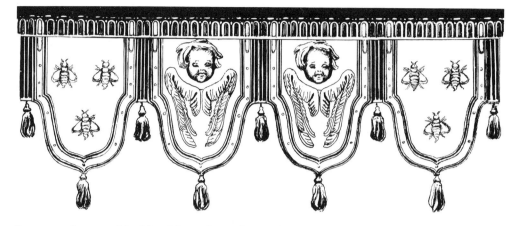

Bronze valance of baldacchino. Opposite: Bernini baldacchino (beneath the central dome of St. Peter's).

Putti with tiara and keys atop baldacchino

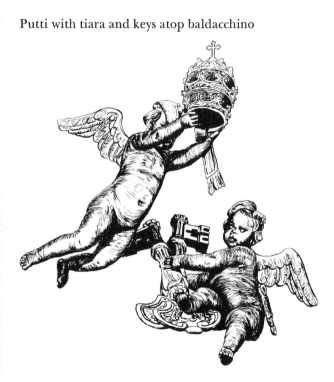

The huge baldacchino was finished in 1633 and dedicated on June 29, the feast day of the Apostle Peter. It was constructed at a cost of more than 200,000 scudi and required 93 tons of bronze, some of which was taken from the dome of St. Peter's and the roof and porch ceiling of the Pantheon. The dynamic open-work canopy, profusely adorned with sculpture, rises to an over-all height of almost 100 feet. Its lofty spiral columns, modeled after those of the ancient Constantinian canopy, are luxuriantly decorated with foliage and *putti*. They stand upon pedestals which bear the coat of arms of Urban VIII, and are joined together at the top by a clothlike, bronze pendanted valance. Pairs of putti over the valance hold tiara and Keys of St. Peter—the papal insignia—and sword and book—the symbols of St. Paul. Above the columns, giant angels clad in swirling drapery hold ropelike garlands attached to the four gently curved scrolls that crown the structure and support an elaborate entablature surmounted by a golden orb and cross.

St. Veronica (Mochi)   St. Helena (Bolgi)

Soon after Urban VIII chose Bernini to design and erect the colossal baldacchino, he conceived the idea of bringing to a central position under the dome the
most sacred relics of the Church. These are: the Veil of St. Veronica, the True
Cross of St. Helena, the Lance of St. Longinus, and the Head of St. Andrew; the
latter, encased in a gold reliquary, was returned in 1964 on orders of Pope Paul
VI, to Patrus, Greece, the city where St. Andrew was beheaded. By the end of
1629, Pope Urban had resolved to have monumental, 16-foot high statues of those
saints placed in the pier niches, and balconies built above, where the relics could
be exhibited on special holy days. In December, Bernini and three other prominent sculptors were selected to do the statues, first in stucco, later in marble.
Bernini received the commission for St. Longinus, a nine-year project which he

St. Longinus (Bernini)   St. Andrew (Duquesnoy)

finished in 1638, and received silver in payment, amounting to about $3,300.

Simultaneously with his work on the Longinus, Bernini designed and directed the execution of: Pope Urban VIII's tomb, (1628-1647); the tomb of Countess Matilda, (1633-1637); and the large marble relief of the *Pasce Oves Meas*, (1633-1637), which was placed inside the portico over Filarete's bronze doors in 1649. During this same period, between 1633 and 1640, Bernini also supervised the construction of the pier balconies and their stairways, hollowed within the massive pillars. He designed the four balcony-shrines with white marble pictorials of angels and putti bearing representations of the relics. They are backed by varicolored marble and flanked by the venerated spiral columns from Constantine's basilica. The spaces above the pictorials are filled with billowy cloud formations and cherubs.

79

The only serious mistake Bernini made in his long prolific career was in accepting, in 1637, Pope Urban's commission to design bell towers for the completion of the work that had been started by Maderna and abandoned in 1621. Bernini proposed lordly campaniles that were to be about 330 feet high, formed of three columnated tiers, crested by spires adorned with pairs of winged victories. The first tower was erected, on the south side, but in a very short time its previously built substructure began to settle, causing a strain on the façade so that cracks appeared in the portico. Construction was halted in 1641, then in 1646 the tower was torn down and Urban VIII's successor, Pope Innocent X (1644-1655), removed Bernini from his position as chief architect. The four winged victories, executed between 1640 and 1642 by Bernini's brother, Luigi, were afterwards placed above the third arch of both side aisles of the nave where they grace Innocent X's coat of arms.

Right: Old engraving showing Bernini's bell tower before demolition

Left: Bernini's bell tower

Bernini's elevation of façade of St. Peter's
with proposed bell towers

More than a century and a quarter later, Pope Pius VI (1775-1799) commissioned Valdier to design the present clocks, with church bells below that weigh almost ten tons, in place of the ill-fated towers. These ornate timepieces, mounted between angels and topped by the papal insignia, were cast in Germany and added to the façade in 1782. Although Bernini was demoted to a subordinate post, and remained in disfavor with Innocent X, he was allowed to go ahead with the decoration of chapels and nave pilasters which the Pope had commissioned him to do in 1645.

Bernini planned to enrich the sides of the pilasters beneath the arches with three-dimensional symbolic forms set against a background of polychrome marble. For these parts he designed pairs of animated putti holding up medallions with carved portraits of early martyred popes and others, like those of the colossal baldacchino, carrying the papal insignia and the emblems of St. Paul. He also suggested the reclining stucco statues, representing Christian virtues, that occupy the interspaces above the nave arches. To execute this detailed project, Bernini engaged altogether thirty-nine sculptors and masons, and by 1649 the ornamentation of the pilasters was complete.

Clock towers of St. Peter's.

Nave decorations of St. Peter's.

During the final years of Innocent X's reign, Bernini's numerous craftsmen were employed to finish the task of facing walls with marble and marbled stucco. It was then discovered that dampness was having a detrimental effect on the frescoes and oil paintings above the altars. Soon after, the decision was made to replace the original masterpieces with imperishable mosaic copies. The accurate, jewel-like reproductions, of which there are thirty or more, were done almost entirely by artisans of the papal mosaic factory over a long period of time extending up through the first half of the eighteenth century. The most impressive one is the enlarged copy of Raphael's *Transfiguration*, made by Pozzi who spent ten years on the work. It is placed over the Altar of the Transfiguration, on the east side of the Pier of St. Andrew. Also noteworthy are three great mosaics executed by Fabio Christoforo and his son, Pietro Paolo. These are: Guercino's *St. Petronilla*, over the altar dedicated to that saint in the Chapel of St. Michael; Carlo Maratta's *Baptism of Our Lord*, in the Baptismal Chapel; and Domenichino's *Last Communion of St. Jerome*, on the east side of the Pier of St. Longinus.

Alexander VII (1655-1667) reinstated Bernini as chief architect and commissioned him, in 1656, to design the majestic semi-circular colonnades surrounding the vast Piazza di San Pietro, and the glorified Cathedra in the west apse which enshrines the actual venerated chair that is believed to have been once used by St. Peter.

Details of the Altar of the Transfiguration and the mosaic copy of Raphael's *Transfiguration*

Domenichino's *Last Communion of St. Jerome*

Pope Alexander laid the foundation stone of the travertine colonnades on August 28, 1657, and saw them essentially completed before his death ten years later. They are formed in two great arcs connected to slanted corridors which give the entrance court a keyhole shape, 1,110 feet long and 650 feet wide in its greatest breadth. Their height of 64 feet was determined by the need to retain a view of the windows of the papal apartment in the Vatican Palace from which the Pope gives his blessing to the people gathered in the Piazza.

Bernini chose the simple, sturdy Tuscan Order for the columns of his colonnades to contrast with, and thereby accentuate, the slender Corinthian columns of the basilica's huge façade. There are altogether 284 of these massive columns and 88 pillars, all 52 feet high, arranged in four rows with the spaces between providing three covered passageways on both sides of the Piazza. The center aisle of each colonnade, originally intended for horse-drawn coaches, is about as wide as a two-lane street. The columns carry an Ionic entablature, surmounted by a balustrade on which stand 96 travertine statues of saints and martyrs, 12 feet tall, designed by Bernini. The figures atop the corridors, executed more than twenty years after the death of Bernini, during the reign of Clement XI (1700-1721), bring the total number to 164.

In conjunction with his work on the colonnades, Bernini skillfully transformed the principal entrance to the Papal Palace, a constricted tapering ramp, into a grand ceremonial staircase. This is the Scala Regia, or Royal Stairs, constructed between 1663 and 1666. It begins at the level of the portico of St. Peter's and leads in two flights to the Sala Regia, the Hall of the Seven Doors, which is a large impressive anteroom with entrances to the Sistine and Pauline Chapels. The main landing of the staircase, adjoining the north end of the portico, is decorated with beautiful stucco work forming ceiling medallions which depict the baptism of Constantine, and the Emperor laying the foundation stone of the first basilica. The papal coat of arms is displayed above the arch of the staircase between two heralding figures of Fame. Bernini's monumental equestrian statue of Constantine, commissioned by Innocent X in 1654 and finished in 1668, was placed on the right side of the landing in 1670.

Left: Scala Regia. Below: Bernini's statue of Emperor Constantine.

At the same time Bernini planned the colonnades he made preliminary sketches for the Cathedra, the bishop's seat. He visioned it as a marvelous throne scenographically united to the great baldacchino and, viewed from the church entrance, it appears in the distance dramatically framed by the canopy's giant, blackish spiral columns. But his first conception of the bronze and gilt reliquary, accepted by the Pope in March, 1657, was classical and modestly scaled, being only somewhat larger than the flanking tombs of Paul III and Urban VIII. Although a large model was in construction in 1658, the design passed through several stages of development before its present form was ultimately determined by Bernini and his collaborators in 1661. It had evolved into an overwhelming creation set beneath a spectacular golden "Glory" of angels, cherubs, surging clouds and radiant sunburst, illuminated by a circular stained glass window with the symbolic Dove of the Holy Spirit.

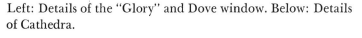

Left: Details of the "Glory" and Dove window. Below: Details of Cathedra.

95

Four huge bronze statues of the Fathers of the Church—Saints Ambrose, Augustine, Athanasius, and Chrysostom—all over 16 feet tall, hold the Cathedra aloft; two angels grace its sides; and putti lightly rest at the top, holding up the tiara and Keys of St. Peter. On the high back of this splendid throne is a relief of the *Pasce Oves Meas* by Bernini; two others he designed, *Handing Over of the Keys to St. Peter*, and *Washing of the Feet*, are on the sides below the seat; other parts are lavishly embellished with floral motifs. By 1633 the throne and statues had been cast, yet the polishing and gilding of intricate details continued through December, 1665. In January, 1666, the extraordinary Cathedra was unveiled.

Left: The Cathedra with the "Glory" and Dove window.
Right: Statue of St. Augustine.

Bernini's work on the decoration of St. Peter's, altogether an astonishing and complex series of enterprises, was climaxed with the execution of the colonnades and Cathedra, which most authorities consider to be his greatest accomplishments. Of the two incomparable projects, Bernini's son, Domenico, wrote that they were intended to be the "beginning and end of the magnificence of that great church, and the eye is as much infatuated at the beginning on entering the square as at

the end on seeing the Cathedra." The colonnades have often been described as the welcoming outstretched arms of the church, and Bernini himself referred to them in the same way, adding that they symbolically "embrace Catholics to reinforce their belief, heretics to re-unite them with the Church, and agnostics to enlighten them with the true faith."

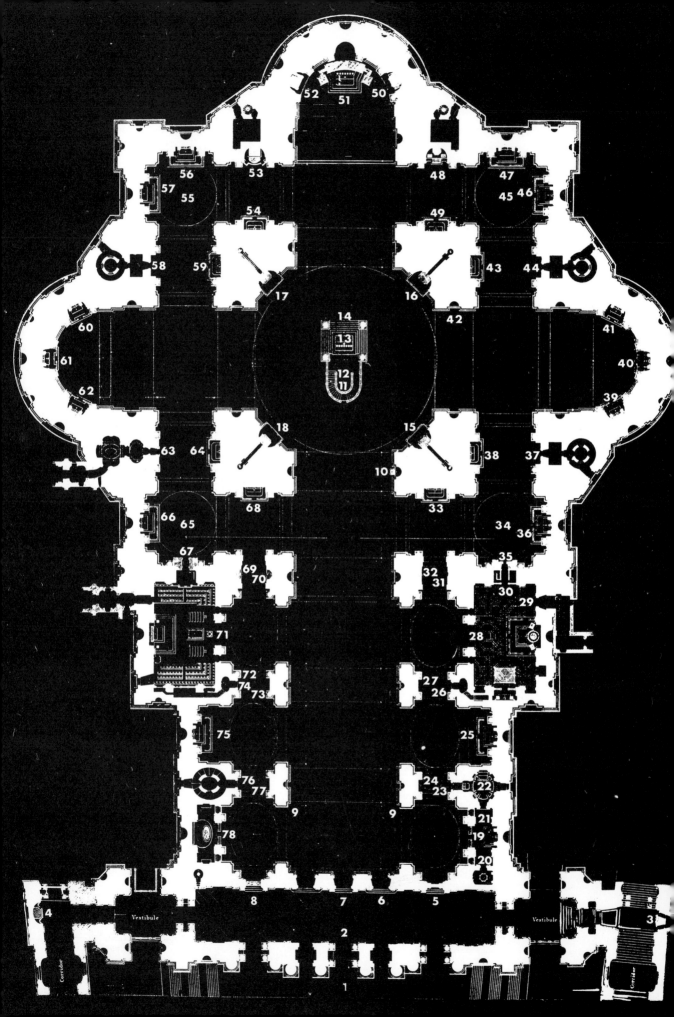

A Guide to the Basilica

1. MADERNA'S FAÇADE
2. NAVICELLA, the restored mosaic of *St. Peter Walking on the Waves*, attributed to Giotto.
3. STATUE OF EMPEROR CONSTANTINE by Bernini.
4. STATUE OF EMPEROR CHARLEMAGNE by Cornacchini.
5. PORTA SANTA, the Holy Door, is kept sealed except during the Holy years which usually occur once every twenty-five years.
6. DOORS OF THE SACRAMENTS have reliefs showing the seven sacraments of the Roman Catholic Church. They were executed by Veranzo Crocetti and installed in 1965.
7. FILARETE'S BRONZE DOORS, opened only when the Pope enters the basilica to celebrate Mass or preside at special ceremonies. Above is Bernini's marble relief of the *Pasce Oves Meas* which depicts the Saviour confiding his flock to St. Peter.
8. BRONZE DOORS OF DEATH by Giacomo Manzù, hung in the portal in June, 1964, show the Virgin Mary being lifted up toward heaven by two angels and Christ as he was lowered from the cross. In eight panels below are scenes depicting death in modern times and others taken from ancient church history.
9. HOLY WATER STOUPS, supported by chubby cherubs about seven feet tall, were designed and executed by Francesco Moderati and Giuseppi Lironi.
10. BRONZE STATUE OF ST. PETER, brought to its site on the south side of the Pier of St. Longinus by Pope Paul V, is believed to be the work of Arnolfo di Cambia, done in the thirteenth century. The life-size sacred figure, seated on a marble chair and raised on a marble pedestal, has been an object of veneration for so long that the toes of its right foot are worn and shiny from the kisses of millions of worshipers. A brilliant mosaic brackground simulates the pattern of the rich brocade pontifical robes in which the statue is vested every year on June 29, the feast day of Sts. Peter and Paul.
11. MARBLE STATUE OF PIUS VI (1775-1799) by Antonio Canova. The kneeling figure was placed in front of the Chapel of the Tomb, in the curve of the Confessio staircase in 1820 by Pius VI's successor, Pius VII.
12. CONFESSIO, completed by Maderna in 1612, is a sunken, semi-circular area in front of the papal altar, enclosed by a marble balustrade and illuminated by

Navicella, attributed to Giotto

95 perpetually burning votive lamps. A double flight of marble stairs leads
down to the chapel over the grave of St. Peter.

13. HIGH ALTAR or Altar of Confession, where, as a general rule, only the Pope
celebrates Mass, stands directly over the Tomb of St. Peter. The almost plain
marble altar, open on all sides, was built by Della Porta between 1592 and
1594 and consecrated by Pope Clement VIII on June 26, 1594.

14. BALDACCHINO, bronze and gilt canopy over the papal altar and Tomb of St.
Peter, was designed by Bernini and dedicated by Pope Urban VIII on June
29, 1633. For a detailed description see page 76.

15. MARBLE STATUE OF ST. LONGINUS with the sacred Lance, about 16 feet high,
was designed and executed by Bernini. The balcony above serves as a gallery
from which privileged visitors are allowed to witness special celebrations.
Over the arched doorway, as on the other pier balconies, are white marble
figures of angels and cherubs set against a polychrome background. Here they
carry an image of the Lance.

16. MARBLE STATUE OF ST. HELENA, mother of Constantine the Great, holding
the Cross, was designed and executed by Bolgi. A pictorial of the Exaltation
of the Cross is on the balcony overhead.

The Holy Door

17. MARBLE STATUE OF ST. VERONICA displaying the miraculous Veil etched with
    the likeness of the Saviour, by Mocchi. The three great relics—a large piece of
    the True Cross, the Veil of St. Veronica, and the spearhead of the holy Lance
    of St. Longinus—are kept in the balcony-shrine above, where they are ex-
    posed for veneration during Holy Week. The pictorial depicts an angel in
    flight bearing the Veil, supported by putti.

18. MARBLE STATUE OF ST. ANDREW by Duquesnoy, representing the crucifixion
    of the saint. Until 1964, when it was returned to Patrus, Greece, the Head of
    St. Andrew was kept in a gold reliquary in the balcony over his statue, from
    which it was exhibited each year on June 14 and November 30. The balcony
    pictorial shows an angel and putti upholding St. Andrew's cross.

19. MICHELANGELO'S PIETÀ, executed in marble in 1498, is the main adornment
    of the Chapel of Our Lady of Pity, the first chapel on the right aisle, near the
    Holy Door. This celebrated devotional masterpiece, the only work Michel-
    angelo ever signed, was placed here in the second half of the seventeenth cen-
    tury beneath a large marble cross. The ceiling of the chapel is decorated with
    The Triumph of the Cross by Lanfranco.

20. COLONNA SANTA, on the right side of the Chapel of Our Lady of Pity, is a

103

Transfiguration (Raphael)

spiral column of white marble, venerated as the one Christ leaned against when disputing with the Doctors in the Temple at Jerusalem. It was enclosed in its protecting marble balustrade by Cardinal Orsini in 1438.

21. SARCOPHAGUS made for Probus, the Christian Prefect of Rome in 395, is on the left side of the Chapel of Our Lady of Pity.

22. CHAPEL OF THE CRUCIFIX, designed by Bernini, is dedicated to St. Nicholas who was Bishop of Myra (Lycia) in the early fourth century and is the original Santa Claus, patron saint of children. A large wooden crucifix, done by Cavallini in the fourteenth century, hangs over the tabernacle at the altar, and above it is a mosaic of St. Nicholas.

23. MONUMENT OF LEO XII (1823-1829), designed and executed by De Fabri in 1835, is raised high on a pedestal and depicts the tall, lean figure of the Pontiff in the act of benediction.

24. MONUMENT OF QUEEN CHRISTINA OF SWEDEN (1626-1689), whose remains are interred in the crypt of St. Peter's, was designed by Carlo Fontana and installed in 1702. The upper part consists of a large circular medallion with a raised profile portrait of the Queen, beneath which is a plaque inscribed with a record of her formal reception into the Church, her funeral in the basilica,

Monument and tomb of Urban VIII (Bernini)

and the dedication of the memorial by Pope Clement XI. On an empty sarcophagus below rests an image of the crown she gave up in 1654. Two cherubs flank the sarcophagus on which there is a bas-relief by John Teudon portraying the Queen's solemn renunciation of Protestantism.

25. CHAPEL OF ST. SEBASTIAN, patron saint of archers, who was a guardsman of the Imperial Palace and slain in 284 during the persecution under Emperor Diocletian by being tied to a tree and shot at with arrows, then flogged to death. Above the altar is a mosaic of the *Martyrdom of St. Sebastian*, copied from a fresco done by Domenichino in 1629. (Monument to Pius XI is on the right side of this chapel.)

26. MONUMENT OF INNOCENT XII (1691-1700), designed by Fillippo della Valle, was erected over the entrance to Innocent's tomb in 1724. It depicts the aged Pope seated on a throne in full pontificals and wearing the tiara, his hand lifted in the gesture of benediction. Below, on either side of the tomb, are statues of Charity and Justice.

27. MONUMENT AND TOMB OF THE COUNTESS MATILDA OF TUSCANY (1046-1115), whose remains were brought to Rome in 1635 on orders of Pope Urban VIII, was designed by Bernini and unveiled in 1637. The graceful, over life-size fig-

105

Monument and tomb of Paul III
(G. della Porta)

ure of the matronly Countess stands erect atop her sarcophagus accompanied
by four cherubs. A relief on the sarcophagus, with figures half life-size, portrays the absolution of Emperor Henry IV by Pope Gregory VII in 1077.

28. CHAPEL OF THE BLESSED SACRAMENT, where the eucharist is enshrined in Bernini's beautiful gilt-bronze tabernacle, is richly surfaced with colored marbles
and lapis lazuli, and closed by an iron grille. The adoring bronze angels,
over life-size, flank the tabernacle with its figures of Christ and the twelve
Apostles; designed by Bernini, they were cast by Girolamo Lucenti between
1673 and 1674. Pietro da Cortona's representation of the *Holy Trinity* is over
the altar, executed in 1669, and on the right, or east wall, is a stigmata pictorial of St. Francis of Assisi by Domenichino.

29. DOOR TO THE ROYAL STAIRCASE, on the left side of the Altar of the Blessed
Sacrament. It is used by the Pope on the occasions when he does not make
a ceremonial entrance through the central portal.

30. DOOR TO THE ORGAN LOFT.

31. MONUMENT AND TOMB OF GREGORY XIII (1572-1585) was designed and executed by Camillo Rusconi between 1719 and 1725. The white marble
monument shows the Pope enthroned on the sarcophagus, his hand raised

Monument and tomb of Alexander
VII (Bernini)

in blessing. On one side a figure of Courage lifts up the pall of the sarcophagus to study the bas-relief of Gregory giving his reformed calendar to the astronomers; on the other side, a figure of Religion holds the Bible.

32. TOMB OF GREGORY XIV (1590-1591), who reigned just ten months, is a simple urn placed in the niche opposite the monument of Gregory XIII.

33. ALTAR OF ST. JEROME, on the east side of the Pier of St. Longinus, has over it an enlarged mosaic copy of Domenichino's celebrated *Last Communion of St. Jerome*, executed by Fabio Christoforo and his son, Pietro Paolo.

34. GREGORIAN CHAPEL, so-named because it was built during the reign of Gregory XIII, although the Pontiff dedicated it to Our Lady of Help in 1578. Constructed by Della Porta, from Michelangelo's design, it is adorned with gold, mosaics, and costly marbles.

35. MONUMENT AND TOMB OF GREGORY XVI (1831-1846), designed and executed by Amici, is flanked by figures of Faith and Charity. On the front of the sepulchral memorial is a bas-relief celebrating the reunion of the Armenian and other Eastern churches with Rome.

36. ALTAR OF OUR LADY OF SUCCOR, over which hangs the famous, ancient painting of the Madonna del Soccorso. Beneath the altar, in a green marble sar-

107

Monument and tomb of Innocent VIII
(Piero and Antonio Pollaiolo)

cophagus, are the ashes of St. Gregory Nazianzen (330-390) entombed there in
1580.

37. MONUMENT AND TOMB OF BENEDICT XIV (1740-1758), designed and executed
by Pietro Bracci, depicts the Pontiff arrayed in papal vestments standing over
his sarcophagus in the act of benediction. Below are figures of Wisdom and
Humility.

38. ALTAR OF ST. BASIL, on the north side of the Pier of St. Longinus, over which
is a reproduction of the *Mass of St. Basil* by Subleyras.

39. ALTAR OF ST. WENCESLAUS, Duke of Bohemia, with a mosaic copy of Carou-
selli's painting of St. Wenceslaus above.

40. ALTAR OF STS. PROCESSUS AND MARTINIAN, the jailers of St. Peter who became
his converts and were baptized by the Apostle, has over it a mosaic of Valen-
tin's painting of their martyrdom in the first century.

41. ALTAR OF ST. ERASMUS, his martyrdom depicted in mosaic, is a reproduction
of a painting by Poussin.

42. STATUE OF ST. BRUNO, executed in 1744 by M. Slodiz, represents the saint in
the austere garb of a Carthusian Monk—the order he founded in 1084—re-
fusing the award of the bishop's miter and staff.

108

Bernini's tabernacle

43. ALTAR OF THE NAVICELLA, on the north side of the Pier of St. Helena, has over it a mosaic copy of Lanfranco's painting of the *Saviour Walking on the Waters*.

44. MONUMENT AND TOMB OF CLEMENT XIII (1758-1769), designed and executed by A. Canova, unveiled in 1795. The statue of the Pontiff kneeling in prayer, with his tiara in front of him, is fixed on a base of gray marble. On the right sits the Angel of Death, head leaning against an inverted torch; on the left Religion stands holding a cross. Below, two lions guard the door leading to the vault.

45. CHAPEL OF ST. MICHAEL THE ARCHANGEL

46. ALTAR OF ST. MICHAEL before which are buried the remains of Julius II (1503-1513) and Sixtus IV (1471-1484), interred there in 1928 after removal from the Chapel of the Blessed Sacrament. Above the altar is a mosaic copy of Guido Reni's painting of St. Michael conquering the devil.

47. ALTAR OF ST. PETRONILLA has over it a mosaic reproduction of Guercino's *Funeral of St. Petronilla* done by Fabio Christoforo and Pietro Paolo. A sarcophagus containing the ashes of the saint is beneath the altar.

48. MONUMENT AND TOMB OF CLEMENT X (1670-1676), designed and executed

by Ercola Ferrata and Matteo Rossi, depicts the Pontiff enthroned over his tomb in the act of giving a blessing. The figures of Clemency and Benignity are at the sides, and below is a bas-relief celebrating the opening of the Holy Door.

49. ALTAR OF ST. PETER, on the west side of the Pier of St. Helena opposite the monument to Clement X, has above it a mosaic reproduction of Costanzi's painting of *St. Peter Resurrecting Tabitha.*

50. MONUMENT AND TOMB OF URBAN VIII (1623-1644) designed by Bernini in 1627, was not completed until 1647. The bronze and gilt statue of the Pope, raised on a high marble plinth, portrays him seated, wearing the tiara and ceremonial attire, his arm lifted in an attitude of benediction. Below sits the figure of Death, a winged skeleton of gilded bronze which appears to have emerged from the bronze and black marble sarcophagus, inscribing the name Urbanus VIII on his register of the deceased. Two white marble statues, twice life-size, lean against the tomb. On the left, Charity carries a sleeping baby; on the right, Justice upholds a sword.

51. CATHEDRA OF ST. PETER, designed by Bernini and completed in 1665, is a grand bronze and gilt reliquary which enshrines the venerated chair of the Apostle, set beneath an astonishing gilt and stucco "Glory" of colossal proportions. For a detailed description, see pages 95 and 97.

52. MONUMENT AND TOMB OF PAUL III (1534-1549), designed and executed by Giacomo della Porta under the guidance of Michelangelo, is considered to be one of the finest monuments in St. Peter's. Completed about 1577 and placed near the Pier of St. Longinus, it was moved to its present site, left of the Cathedra, in 1628. The bronze statue of the Pope, seated on a bronze chair giving the benediction, is raised on a high marble base. Below are reclining marble figures of Prudence, on the right, holding a book in one hand and a mirror in the other; and Justice, on the left, holding a torch. The latter, said to be an image of the Pontiff's sister-in-law, was carved almost nude and received so much criticism that Lorenzo Bernini was commissioned to drape it in a tunic of bronze painted to match the marble statue.

53. MONUMENT AND TOMB OF ALEXANDER VIII (1689-1691) was designed and executed by Bertoni and De Rossi. The bronze, seated statue of the Pontiff is placed on a pedestal, high above his sarcophagus, on which there is a relief commemorating the canonization of five holy persons. The marble figures of Prudence and Religion are on the sides.

54. ALTAR OF THE CRIPPLE, dedicated to Sts. Peter and John, has over it a mosaic reproduction of Mancini's painting of *St. Peter Healing a Cripple.*

55. CHAPEL DELLA COLONNA, or Place of the Five Leos.

56. ALTAR OF ST. LEO (440-461) who successfully halted the invasion of Attila, the "Scourge of God," and his army of Huns in 452. The great marble relief, *The Retreat of Attila,* which perpetuates the historical event was carved by Algardi and erected over the altar in 1653. The ashes of Leo the Great are contained in a sarcophagus beneath the altar, and the remains of Leo XII (1823-1829) lie in a vault before it.

57. ALTAR OF THE MADONNA DELLA COLONNA, Our Lady of the Pillar, received its name from a representation of the Madonna and the Infant Jesus done on a pillar of the Holy Door of the first St. Peter's. Beneath the altar, in a single sarcophagus carved with the images of the Saviour and the Apostles, are three urns containing the ashes of: Leo II (682-683), Leo III (795-816), and Leo IV (847-855).

58. MONUMENT AND TOMB OF ALEXANDER VII (1655-1667), designed by Bernini, shows the Pope kneeling in prayer clad in a voluminous cape that partly obscures the tiara placed at his side. The marble statue, over life-size, is set on a small rounded pedestal above a large drapery of red marble. Below, the gilt-bronze skeleton of Death can be seen leaping from the entrance to the tomb with an hourglass clutched in his hand. The marble figure of Charity holding a child is on the left; that of Truth, her foot resting on the world, is on the right.

59. ALTAR OF STS. PETER AND PAUL has above it Francesco Vanni's representation of the *Fall of Simon Magus,* a sorcerer who tried to buy spiritual power from the Apostles.

60. ALTAR OF ST. THOMAS over which is a mosaic copy of Camucinni's painting, *The Doubting Thomas.*

61. ALTAR OF THE CRUCIFIXION OF ST. PETER, so-named because of the mosaic reproduction of Guido Reni's painting *The Crucifixion of St. Peter* above it, is dedicated to the martyred Apostles, Sts. Simon and Jude, whose relics are under the altar. Before the altar is the grave of Giovanni da Palestrina, a noted sixteenth century Italian composer of church music.

62. ALTAR OF STS. MARTIAL AND VALERIA has over it a mosaic copy of Spadarino's painting, the *Martyrdom of Valeria.* In front of the altar is the grave of St. Leo IX (1049-1054).

63. MONUMENT AND TOMB OF PIUS VIII (1829-1830), designed by Tenerani, is above the entrance to the sacristy and shows the Pontiff in prayer, kneeling before a figure of the Saviour.

64. ALTAR OF STS. PETER AND ANDREW, on the south side of the Pier of St. Andrew, is also known as the Altar of the Lie, for over it is a mosaic of Roncalli's painting which depicts the death of Sapphira who lied to St. Peter.

65. CLEMENTINE CHAPEL, constructed under the direction of Della Porta, was

completed during the reign of Pope Clement VIII and opened in 1600. The mosaics of the vaulting, by Provenzale, represent the Doctors of the Church.

66. ALTAR OF ST. GREGORY THE GREAT (590-604), beneath which lie his remains encased in a sarcophagus of porphyry. Above the altar is a mosaic reproduction of the *Miracle of St. Gregory* by Sacchi.

67. MONUMENT AND TOMB OF PIUS VII (1800-1823), designed and executed by Bertel Thorvaldsen, depicts the Pope in the act of benediction, seated on a throne placed high above the door of his tomb. Below, at the sides, are the figures of Time and History.

68. ALTAR OF THE TRANSFIGURATION, on the east side of the Pier of St. Andrew, over which is the famous mosaic copy of Raphael's painting of *The Transfiguration of Our Lord*. The great work was executed over a period of ten years by Pozzi who made the reproduction ten times larger than the original.

69. MONUMENT OF LEO XI (1605-1605), who reigned only twenty-six days, is entirely of white marble. It was designed by Algardi who carved the statue of the seated Pope, the sarcophagus it is placed upon, and the bas-relief which depicts the King of France, Henry IV, signing a treaty of peace with Spain. The figures of Majesty and Liberality, standing at the sides of the monument, are credited to Peroni and Ferrata.

70. MONUMENT AND TOMB OF INNOCENT XI (1676-1689) designed by Maratta and executed by Monnot who placed the statue of the enthroned Pope on a high pedestal on which is a narrative relief of John III, King of Poland, driving the Turks out of Vienna in 1683. Below, at the sides of the bronze, scroll-decorated sarcophagus are the figures of Religion and Justice.

71. CHAPEL OF THE CHOIR, its interior designed by Della Porta, has choir stalls for the clergy on each side. Above the altar is a mosaic reproduction of Pietro Bianchi's painting of the *Immaculate Conception*, with twelve diamond stars set into the crown of the Holy Virgin. Beneath the chapel are the remains of Clement XI (1700-1721).

72. MONUMENT OF ST. PIUS X (1903-1914) who was canonized in 1954, is a simple marble representation of the Pontiff and was erected in 1923.

73. MONUMENT AND TOMB OF INNOCENT VIII (1484-1492), designed and executed by Piero and Antonio Pollaiolo a few years after the Pope's death, is the oldest papal monument in St. Peter's. It is entirely of bronze, with two statues of the Pontiff. One represents him seated on a throne, right hand lifted in blessing, left hand holding the Holy Lance; the other shows him in death, lying upon his sarcophagus. In shallow niches on either side of the monument are small figures symbolizing the four Cardinal Virtues: Prudence, Justice, Temperance and Fortitude.

74. TEMPORARY TOMB FOR DECEASED POPES is a bronze vault high above a door

against the wall between the Chapel of the Choir and the Chapel of the Presentation, in which the late pontiff is interred until the completion of a permanent tomb.

75. CHAPEL OF THE PRESENTATION, dedicated to the Mother of God in commemoration of her presentation in the Temple at three years of age. A mosaic reproduction of the *Presentation of the Virgin* by Romanelli is over the altar.

76. MONUMENT OF MARIA CLEMENTINA SOBIESKI (1703-1735) who was the wife of the Stuart Prince James III, mother of Prince Charles Edward and Prince Henry Benedict (the Cardinal-Duke of York), is above the doorway leading to the dome elevator. It was designed by Barigioni and executed by Bracci and consists of a medallion with a mosaic portrait of Maria, supported by the figure of Genius. Her sarcophagus is of porphyry with alabaster drapery.

77. MONUMENT OF THE STUARTS: James III (1688-1766), Charles Edward (1720-1788), and Henry Benedict (1725-1807), directly opposite the monument of Maria Clementina Sobieski, was erected in 1819. The memorial, designed and executed by Canova is made up of a shaft of marble inscribed with a dedication to the last of the Stuarts. Over the inscription are the busts of Charles Edward, left; Henry, Cardinal York, center; and James III, right. Above is the Royal Arms of Great Britain.

78. BAPTISTERY, designed by Carlo Fontana, contains a large font with a cover of red porphyry, believed by some historians to have come from Hadrian's tomb. Mosaic reproductions of *St. Peter Baptising the Centurion*, the *Baptism of St. Processus and St. Martianus*, and Carlo Maratta's *Baptism of Our Lord* decorate the walls of this chapel.

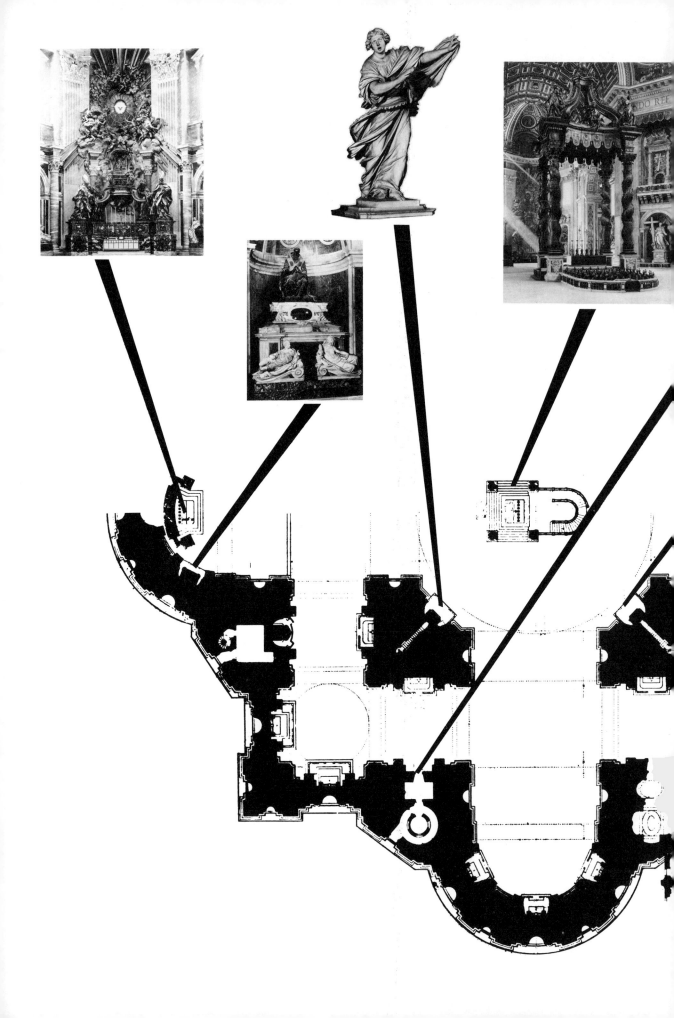

Vestibule

Corridor

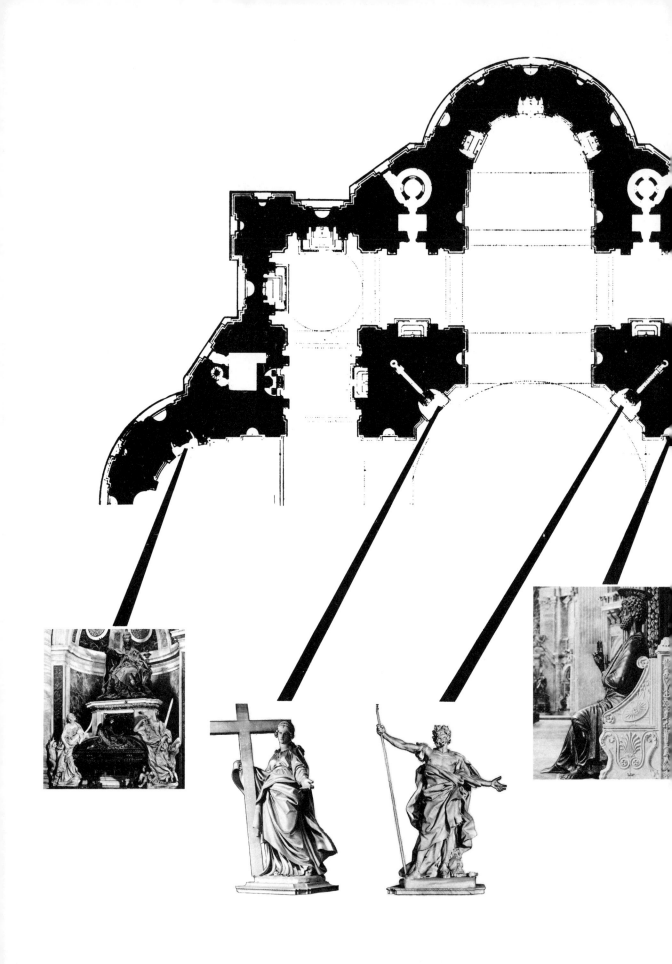

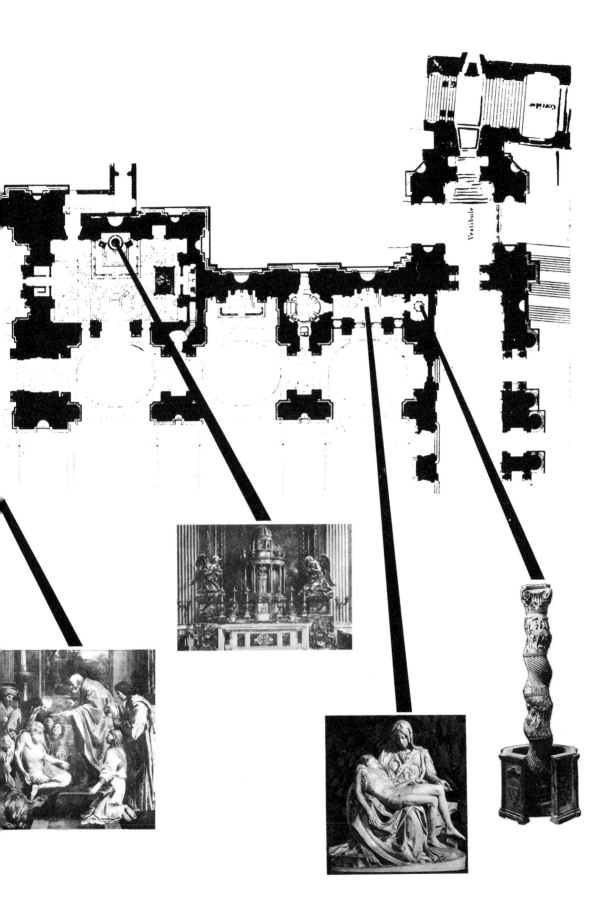

Vestibule

Some Statistics

PIAZZA DI SAN PIETRO

Maximum width	650 feet
Maximum length	1,110 feet

COLONNADES

Height	64 feet
Length of each Arm	306 feet
Number of Columns	284
Number of Pillars	88
Height of Columns and Pillars	52 feet
Number of Statues	164
Height of Statues	12 feet

OBELISK

Weight of Shaft	320 tons
Height of Shaft	82 feet
Height with Base and Cross	132 feet

TWIN FOUNTAINS

Diameter of Octagonal Basins, approximately	28 feet
Height of Water Jets, approximately	46 feet

THE BASILICA, EXTERIOR

Total surface coverage in square feet	227,070
Maximum length	710 feet
Length of Nave and Portico from center of crossing	450 feet
Maximum width across Transepts	500 feet
Height of Columns and Pilasters, over	90 feet
Diameter of Columns	9 feet
Height of Podium	18 feet
Height of Entablature	20 feet
Height of Attic and Balustrade, over	38 feet
Total Height without Façade Statues	167 feet
Number of Façade Statues	12

Height of Façade Statues	19 feet
Width of Façade	375 feet
Height of Portico with Pediment	150 feet
Height of Dome with Lantern and Cross	452 feet
Circumference of Dome at base	630 feet
Height of Order around the Drum	50 feet
Height of Lantern	63 feet
Height and diameter of Bronze Ball	8 feet
Height of Bronze Cross	16 feet

THE BASILICA, INTERIOR

Length from Bronze Door to western Apse Wall	613 feet
Maximum width across Transepts	450 feet
Width of Nave	84 feet
Height of Nave, Sanctuary and Transepts	150 feet
Height of Side Aisles	76 feet
Height of Nave Pilasters	83½ feet
Height of Entablature	20 feet
Height of Dome	335 feet
Diameter of Dome at base	137½ feet
Circumference of Central Piers	240 feet
Height of Pier Statues	16 feet
Height of Baldacchino, approximately	100 feet
Width of Portico	234 feet
Depth of Portico	43½ feet
Height of Portico, approximately	65 feet
Number of Windows	290
Number of Chandeliers	800
Number of Chapels, including those in Sacristy and Crypt	27
Number of Altars, including those in Sacristy and Crypt	48
Number of Statues, including those in Sacristy and Crypt	390
Number of Columns, including those of the exterior	748

Glossary

AMBULATORY—An aisle encircling an apse.

APSE—The termination of a nave, aisle or side chapel, usually semicircular with a half dome.

ATTIC—A low story placed above a cornice.

BALDACCHINO—A canopy over an altar, usually supported by four columns.

BALUSTRADE—A hand-rail supported by a range of small, often vaselike, pillars.

BAROQUE—A term given to a style of art and architecture during the late Renaissance, which was characterized by dynamic opposition and energy and by the use of elaborate carved ornament, scrolls, and curves.

BARREL VAULT—A semicylindrical vault having parallel abutments.

BAS-RELIEF—Sculpture in which the figure projects but slightly from the background.

BAY—A principal compartment or division of a structure as marked off by the piers, pillars, and columns.

BUTTRESS—A projecting structure to support and give stability to a wall or building.

CATHEDRA—A bishop's seat or throne.

CLERESTORY—An upper part of a building which rises clear of the roofs of other parts and whose walls contain windows for lighting the interior.

COFFER—An ornamental panel deeply recessed in the under surface of a vault, dome, or portico ceiling.

COLONNADE—A series or range of columns supporting an entablature.

COLUMN—A kind of supporting pillar of circular section, consisting of a shaft, base, and capital.

CORNICE—The top, projecting part of the entablature.

CROSSING—The point of intersection where the transept crosses the nave in a church.

CRYPT—A vault or chamber under the main floor of the church.

DOME—A hemispherical vault.

DRUM—A vertical circular wall carrying a dome; one of the cylindrical blocks of which the shaft of a column is composed.

ENTABLATURE—The upper part of an order of architecture that rests upon the columns, consisting of an architrave, frieze and cornice.

FAÇADE—The face or front of a building.

FLUTING—A series of grooves, usually vertical, on the shaft of a column or pilaster.

FRESCO—A technique of painting on freshly spread plaster.

LANTERN—An open structure set upon a roof or apex of a dome for ornament or to admit light.

LOGGIA—A roofed open galley.

MEDALLION—A tablet or panel resembling a large medal, bearing a figure, portrait, or ornament, represented in relief.

MOSAIC—Surface decoration formed by small sections of stone, glass, and marble set in cement.

NARTHEX—The portico or outer porch of Early Christian churches.

NAVE—The central hall of a church, usually rising higher than the side aisles.

OCULUS—A round opening at the crown of a dome.

ORDER—The base, shaft, and capital of a column and its entablature.

PEDIMENT—The triangular wall sections above the entablature which supports the sloping roof.

PENDENTIVE—One of the triangular curved sections of vaulting that supports a dome over a square area.

PERISTYLE—A system of columns with entablature surrounding a court or structure.

PIER—A mass of masonry supporting an arch or lintel; also applied to a piece of wall between two openings.

PILASTER—An upright rectangular feature, projecting from a wall and treated as a column, with capital, shaft, and base.

PILLAR—A separate architectural support resembling a column.

PLAN—A diagram drawn to show the shape of a building and the arrangement of its parts on the ground.

PODIUM—A low wall serving as a foundation or substructure for a range of columns.

PORTICO—A porch with roof upheld by columns or piers.

PRESBYTERY—That part of a church reserved for officiating priests.

PUTTI—Sculptured or painted figures of naked Cupid-like children.

RELIEF—The projection of a figure or design from a surface.

RELIQUARY—A box, casket, or shrine for keeping or exhibiting a relic.

RIB—A projecting frame in a vault or arched ceiling.

RINCEAU—A decorative motif consisting of a winding and branching scroll elaborated with leaves and other natural forms.

SACRISTY—A room for vestments and sacred vessels of the church.

TRANSEPT—The arm of a church, projecting at right angles to the main building.

VAULT—An arched covering of masonry over a building or opening.

Bibliography

Ackerman, J. S. *The Architecture of Michelangelo*. London: Zwemmer, 1961

Allsopp, B. *A General History of Architecture*. London: Pitman, 1955

Anichini, G. *La Basilica perdenziana St. Pietro*. Rome: Illustrasione Vaticana, Anno 7, 1936

Atchison, B. *Royal Academy Lectures on St. Peter's*. London: Builder, Vol. 80, 1901

Bach, R. F. *The Dome of St. Peter's in Rome*. New York: The Brickbuilder, Vol. 25, 1916

Begni, R. *The Vatican*. New York: Letters and Arts Publishing Co., 1914

Beissel, S. *Vaticanishe minaturen*. St. Louis: Herder & Co., 1893

Brandes, G. *Michelangelo, His Life*. New York: Frederick Ungar Publishing Co., 1963

Braun, H. *Historical Architecture*. London: Batsford, 1950

Briggs, M. *Architecture in Italy*. New York: E. P. Dutton & Co., 1961

Budden, L. *The Approach to St. Peter's*. England: Town Planning Review, Vol. 7, 1917

Buddensieg, T. *Le Coffret en avoire de Pola*. Paris: Cahiers Archeologiques, No. 10, 1959

Chattard, G. P. *Nuova descrisione de Vaticano*. Rome: Barbellini, 1762

Cocchelli, C. *Il Vaticano*. Rome: Besletti & Tumnimelli, 1927

Conant, K. *Two Designs for the Façade of St. Peter's in Rome*. Washington: Journal of the American Institute of Architects, Vol. 5, 1917

Fattorusso, J. *Wonders of Italy*. Florence: Media Series, 1959

Fletcher, Sir B. *A History of Architecture on the Comparative Method*. New York: Charles Scribner's Sons, 1931

Forsyth, G. *Transept of Old St. Peter's at Rome*. Princeton: 1955

Franklin, J. W. *The Cathedrals of Italy*. New York: Hastings House, 1958

Frey, D. *Das Kuppelmodell Von St. Peter in Rome*. Leipsig: Kunstchchronik und Kunstmarkt, Vol. 57, 1921

Gloag, J. *Guide to Western Architecture*. New York: Macmillan Co., 1958

Hafner, V. *Comparative Notes on Dome of St. Peter's*. Washington: Journal of American Institute of Architects, Vol. 10, 1922

Hamlin, D. *Architecture Through the Ages*. New York: Longmans Green & Co., 1900

Kerschbaum, E. *Tombs of St. Peter and St. Paul*. London: Secher & Warburg, 1959

Kimball, F. *A History of Architecture*. New York: Harper & Brothers, 1918

Letarouilly, P. M. *Le Vatican 1795-1855*. Paris: Simil, 1882

Mariani, V. *Michelangelo*. Rome: Fratelli, 1943

Nogara, B. *Art Treasures of the Vatican*. New York: Tudor Publishing Co., 1950

Perkins, J. *Shrine of St. Peter's and Its Twelve Spiral Columns*. London: Journal of Roman Studies, Vol. 42, 1952

Pisle, S. *Delle Mura e Porte del Vaticano*. Rome: S. Leone, 1834

Potter, M. K. *Art of the Vatican*. Boston: L. C. Page, 1903

Prentice, R. *Heritage of the Cathedral*. New York: William Morrow and Company, 1936

Robb, D. *Art in the Western World*. New York: Harper & Row, 1953

Sladen, D. *How to See the Vatican*. London: K. Paul & French, 1914

Tapié, V. L. *The Age of Grandeur*. New York: Grove Press, Inc., 1960

Upjohn, E. M. *History of World Art*. New York: Oxford University Press, 1949

Van der Veldt, J. *Exploring the Vatican*. London: Hollis & Carter, 1947

Von Matt, L. *Art in the Vatican*. New York: Universe Books, Inc., 1962

Watterson, E. *Architecture*. New York: W. W. Norton & Company, 1950

Wittkower, R. *Bernini, Gian Lorenzo*. London: Phaidon Press Publishers, Inc., 1955

Index

Page numbers enclosed in parentheses indicate pages on which illustrations appear

125

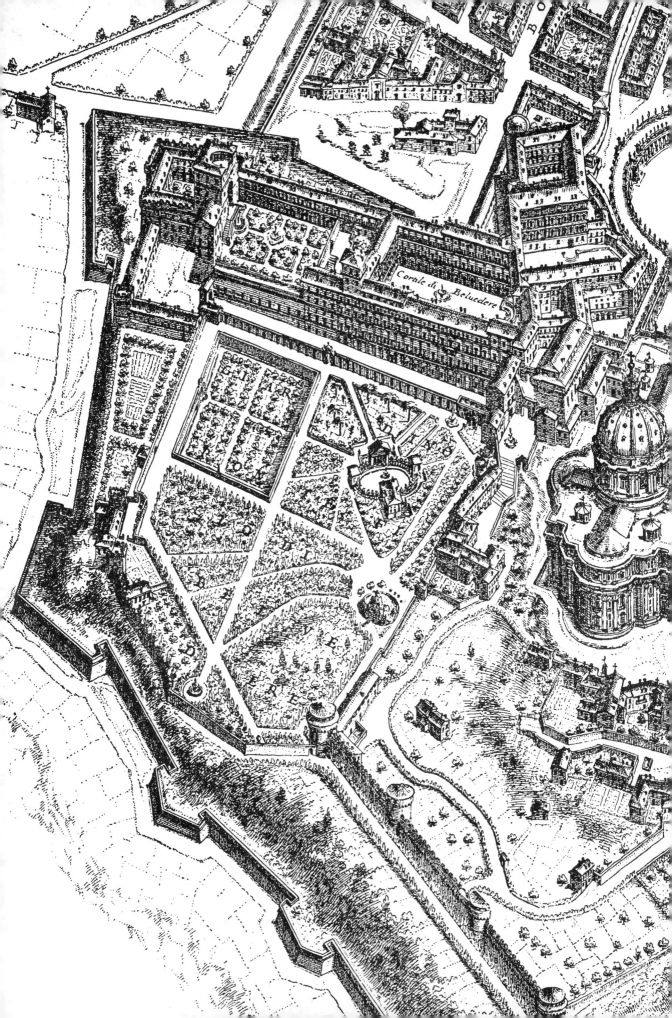
Cortile di Beluedere

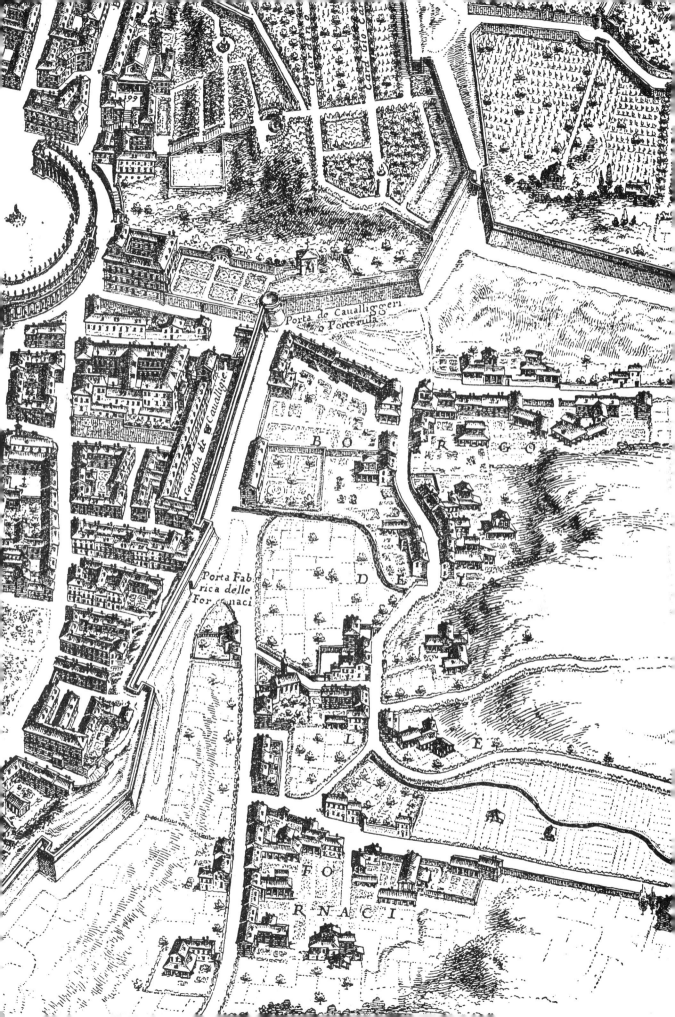

Porta de Caualliggeri o Porterilla

Guardia di Caualligie

Porta Fab rica delle For naci

BO R G O

D E L

L E

FO R NACI